Looking After Children: Research into Practice

The Second Report
to the Department of Health on
Assessing Outcomes in Child Care

Edited by Harriet Ward

London: HMSO

ISBN 0 11 321847 8

Also published by HMSO are the following complementary titles:

Looking After Children: Management and Implementation Guide
ISBN 0 11 321846 X, 1995

Looking After Children: Assessing Outcomes in Child Care
ISBN 0 11 321459 6, 1991

Looking After Children: Good Parenting, Good Outcomes Training Resources
Pack ISBN 0 11 321845 1, 1995

Looking After Children: Research into Practice ISBN 0 11 321847 8, 1995

Looking After Children: Trial Pack ISBN 0 11 321903 2, 1995

Looking After Children: Training Guide ISBN 0 11 321884 2, 1995

Looking After Children: Essential Information Record ISBN 0 11 321849 4, 1995

Looking After Children: Placement Plan ISBN 0 11 321850 8, 1995

Looking After Children: Review ISBN 0 11 321848 6, 1995

Looking After Children: Care Plan ISBN 0 11 321851 6, 1995

Looking After Children: Consultation Papers ISBN 0 11 321852 4, 1995

Assessment and Action Records: under 1 year ISBN 0 11 321854 0, 1995

Assessment and Action Records: 1 and 2 years ISBN 0 11 321855 9, 1995

Assessment and Action Records: 3 and 4 years ISBN 0 11 321856 7, 1995

Assessment and Action Records: 5–9 years ISBN 0 11 321857 5, 1995

Assessment and Action Records: 10–14 years ISBN 0 11 321858 3, 1995

Assessment and Action Records: 15 years and over ISBN 0 11 321859 1, 1995

Contents

**Part
Three:**

**IMPLEMENTING THE ASSESSMENT AND
ACTION RECORDS AS PART OF A
COMPREHENSIVE SYSTEM FOR PLANNING
AND REVIEW**

Chapter 5

**Change in Organisations: Likely Problems in
Implementing *Looking After Children*
Roger Bullock**

Chapter 6

**Research Messages for Implementation
Harriet Ward**

List of Tables

Preface

This book describes the research and development associated with the Department of Health-funded project on assessing outcomes in child care, the current stage of which is entitled *Looking After Children: Good Parenting, Good Outcomes*. The aim of this project is to introduce ideas about outcome into social work practice; it is supported by the following materials, all of which, unless otherwise stated, are published by HMSO:

Looking After Children: Assessment and Action Records (Revised Version)
The six age-related Assessment and Action Records are designed to promote good quality care for the children and young people for whom local authorities share responsibilities. They encourage communication between all those involved in the care of the child. They should be used to assess children's progress in relation to the care they receive and to plan improvements. When completed at regular intervals they provide information about outcomes. If aggregated, these outcome data can be used as a basis for evaluating the service provided and identifying how resources can be more accurately directed.

Looking After Children: Planning and Review Forms (Revised Version)
The Planning and Review forms enable local authorities to fulfil their statutory responsibilities towards all looked after children, including those receiving respite care. They consist of:

Essential Information Record Parts 1 and 2:
Part One provides information needed immediately by carers looking after a child in an unplanned placement. The form is self-duplicating, so that information can be shared with carers at once.

Part Two asks for more comprehensive information about the child or young person's background, including both the legal and the placement history. Both the computerised and the paper-based versions of this form gather the information required for completing the SSDA 903 return required annually by the Department of Health.

Care Plan

The Care Plan ensures that all children and young people looked after have clearly stated objectives set out for their care and a strategy for achieving them.

Placement Plan

The Placement Plan is designed to determine how best a child or young person's day-to-day needs can be met during a placement. It records arrangements for a child's upbringing where responsibilities are divided between a number of people, for instance parents, social workers, foster carers, residential staff and young people themselves.

Part One: Placement Agreement includes the information and agreements which must be completed before a child is placed. It incorporates the immediate agreements to accommodation and medical treatment and records essential names and addresses. The form is self-duplicating so that information can be shared with carers immediately.

Part Two: Day-to-Day Arrangements provides detailed information about the child's everyday routines. It also clarifies contact arrangements.

The Review Form

The Review Form guides the practitioner through the review process outlined in the *Review of Children's Cases Regulations 1991*. It provides a framework for ensuring that the agreed day-to-day arrangements continue to meet a child's needs, that the overall care plan is still appropriate and that the work required to meet its objectives is still being undertaken. It is accompanied by *Consultation Papers*, designed to help young people, parents and carers make their views known at the review meeting.

The *Assessment and Action Records* and the *Planning and Review Forms* were designed by members of the original Department of Health Working Party on Child Care Outcomes and revised by the Looking After Children Research and Development Team based at Dartington Social Research Unit, in association with colleagues from the Universities of Bristol, Bath and Swansea, the National Children's Bureau and other agencies in the child care field, and representatives from local authorities. The work was undertaken in collaboration with the Department of Health and the Department for Education.

The Looking After Children Management and Implementation Guide

This is designed to help managers, planners and social work supervisors set up the *Looking After Children* system and make the best use of it. In addition to guidance for managers and social work supervisors, it also includes information for those who need to extract and analyse data from the completed forms. It includes guidance on setting up the *Looking After Children Computer System* and using data from the Essential Information Record to complete the SSDA 903 return.

The *Management and Implementation Guide* was written and edited by Hilary Corrick, Debbie Jones and Harriet Ward in consultation with the Social Services Research and Development Unit, University of Bath and the Department of Health.

The Looking After Children Training Resources Pack

This contains a training guide, video, reader, practice examples and a copy of the management and implementation guide. Training is aimed at social workers, residential staff and foster carers. The specimen training plan included in these materials recommends that training should be offered either as an intensive two-day course or that it should be integrated into the implementation process and undertaken over a fourteen week period when practitioners are beginning to use the materials in their everyday work.

The *Training Resources Pack* was compiled by Sonia Jackson, University of Swansea and Sue Kilroe, University of Bristol.

Looking After Children Computer System (LACCS)

The Looking After Children Computer System (LACCS) consists of a computerised database which replicates the Essential Information Record. The database offers four modules which provide: records for children currently being looked after; records for other children, such as those in need; an address book; and the facility to compile an SSDA 903 return from the data collected.

The computer system is complemented by the *Looking After Children Data Manual* which contains a technical description of the computerised Essential Information Record and guidance on codes required for the SSDA 903 return.

The *Looking After Children Computer System* was constructed by the Social Services Research and Development Unit (SSRADU), University of Bath, in consultation with the Looking After Children Research and

Development Team and the Department of Health. Further details are available from Social Services Research and Development Unit, The New Church, Henry Street, Bath, BA1 1JR

The *Looking After Children* Research and Development Team would like to thank all the many people who have provided advice and support over the project. The academic team has been complemented by an active group within the Department of Health; we are particularly indebted to Carolyn Davies in the Research and Development Division, who has played a major part in guiding the project and obtaining funding throughout the eight years of its lifetime. We are also grateful for the support given to the project since its beginning from Rupert Hughes in the Community Services Division and Wendy Rose in the Social Services Inspectorate. Without the initiative of these three people, *Looking After Children* would never have advanced from a theoretical concept to a widely-implemented practice tool. The current stage of the project has greatly benefited from the initiative and enthusiasm of Helen Jones in the Social Services Inspectorate, who, while acting as a liaison between the inspectorate and the research team, played a vital role in translating the materials from research into practice and is now managing the implementation team. We also owe thanks to Peter Goldblatt in the Statistics Division, who managed the computerisation aspects of the project and facilitated the link with the SSDA 903 returns. Jane Scott in the Research and Development Division also deserves particular thanks for the extensive work she put in, both in liaising between the Department of Health, the research team and the local authorities and, latterly, as a member of the implementation team. We are also indebted to Elizabeth Hunter Johnston and David Matthews in the Community Services Division who have taken the project up at policy level, and Geoff James, from the Social Services Inspectorate, who provided extensive advice and support until his recent retirement.

We have also benefited from the advice and assistance of numerous academic colleagues, practitioners and managers in local authorities and carers and children who tested out the materials or sat on working parties and advisory groups. Full details of members of the working parties are given in Appendix One. In particular we would like to thank Spencer Millham, Roger Bullock and Michael Little at Dartington Social Research Unit; David Quinton, Roy Parker, Philippa Russell and Ruth Sinclair, who acted as consultants to the project; and Jane Aldgate, Brenda Bullock, Fred Fever, Rob Hutchinson, Barbara Kahan, John Randall, June Thoburn and Peter Thistlethwaite who acted as critical readers. We also owe particular thanks to Kevin Mount, who designed and prepared the materials for publication and to Chris Stone who supervised the various stages of printing and publishing.

None of this project would have come to fruition without the extensive secretarial and administrative support provided by Sue Crook and Sally Watts.

Part One
Introduction

Chapter 1

Introduction

'But what good came of it at last?' asks the little boy in Southey's poem as Old Caspar recounts the story of the battle of Blenheim in the evening sun. It is a question seldom asked in war or child welfare, perhaps because we would rather not hear the answer. *Looking After Children* is an attempt to ask the question in such a way that the answer will lead to better parenting for children looked after away from their families and thus increase the chances of a good outcome for them.

Background

The project began with a working party of policy makers, practitioners and academics, established by the Department of Health (then the DHSS) to consider the question of outcome in child care. The working party produced both a study of the concept of outcome, and also a series of practical instruments designed to introduce these ideas into everyday social work practice. These were published as *Looking After Children: Assessing Outcomes in Child Care*, (Parker *et al* (eds), 1991; Department of Health, 1991a), as part of the series surrounding the implementation of the *Children Act 1989*.

The project might have concluded with the disbanding of the working party in 1991. However, there was considerable interest in both the ideas that underpinned *Looking After Children* and in the practice instruments. Central government policy makers, who had drawn heavily on research in framing the 1989 legislation and guidance, saw the project as an opportunity to encourage local authorities to collect information about the outcomes of their interventions and thus increase their accountability. Managers and practitioners in social services departments saw *Looking After Children* as an opportunity to improve practice and to overhaul their review and monitoring arrangements. Researchers drew upon the project materials because they offered a common methodology that was potentially able to provide comparative data; indeed, an extensive database is emerging from research groups around the world that have adopted the approach.

Widespread interest in the first stage of the project encouraged the Department of Health to engage in a programme of research and development into both the applicability of the *Looking After Children* materials and the issues surrounding their implementation. Additional work began on computerisation and the production of training resources.

This book describes the work undertaken by the *Looking After Children* research and development team between the initial publications and the launch of the revised materials in 1995. In this period, activity has focused as much on development work as it has on research; however the two should not be regarded as separate, for both interact. A major concern has been to ensure that the development work as well as the research is as 'scientific' as possible. Hence, the research team has tested the relevance of the materials to the concerns of ordinary families. Assessments have been made of the quality of care received by a group of 379 children in the community and data from this study have been used to establish some general features of 'normal' parenting behaviour. The extent to which the materials are acceptable—and useful—to social workers, carers, children and young people looked after away from home has also been assessed, from a study group of 204 children in care or accommodation in five local authorities. The project team consulted widely with managers and practitioners in many different agencies and was also able to benefit from the views of numerous parents, children and carers.

In response to the findings of the research and consultation exercises, the original *Looking After Children* materials have been extensively revised; they have also been altered in the light of new child care research and recent changes in legislation. During the course of the work, much has been discovered about the issues to be considered in making practice tools attractive to professionals. We have also reached a better understanding of the conditions necessary to introduce new initiatives to local authorities and other organisations. The findings of these various endeavours are described in the following pages.

The book also provides a justification for local authorities, social workers and researchers who might use the *Looking After Children* materials, in that the approach responds to the frequently expressed objections to this type of work. Evidence shows that the materials are neither as time-consuming nor as costly as some critics have suggested; it also demonstrates how the benefits to be gained from using them increase over time and eventually outweigh the initial expenditure. The book also describes how objections that the original materials were not applicable to children with disabilities or from ethnic minority groups have been taken into account during the revision. Ample evidence is offered to rebut the criticism that the questions asked are too middle class and remote from the situation of disadvantaged children.

The book is divided into four parts. Part One introduces the reader to the principal themes which underpinned the thinking behind the project and gives a comprehensive description of the research and development strategy employed since the original report on outcomes. Part Two looks at the pressures influencing the revisions to the materials, not least the new evidence on standards of parenting by local authorities and ordinary families. Part Three considers the problems of implementing the Assessment and Action Records as part of a comprehensive review system; Part Four looks at the potential of the information produced by the *Looking After Children* approach and demonstrates how the data might be used. The remainder of this chapter summarises the key features and findings of the first stage of the project, as described in the 1991 report.

Why Assess Outcomes?

The Working Party on Child Care Outcomes was set up by the Department of Health and Social Security in April 1987, a time when several factors had combined to undermine public and professional confidence in the child care services. A long series of child abuse inquiries had thrown doubt on the ability of social services departments to safeguard children's well-being even at the most basic level (Reder *et al*, 1993); a growing body of research had begun to identify weaknesses in social work decision-making (e.g. Packman *et al*, 1986; Vernon and Fruin, 1986); the problem of instability in foster care seemed intractable (Berridge and Cleaver, 1987); and the difficulties of offering children a good quality of life in residential care appeared to be increasing (Colton, 1988; Berridge, 1985).

A second issue was the growing significance of consumers: children and young people within the care system and those who had recently left it were beginning to make their voices heard through the Who Cares? movement and the National Association of Young People in Care (Page and Clark, 1977); consumer studies were highlighting the importance of those day-to-day aspects of living away from home which can be overlooked by policy-focused research (Gardner, 1987); the Family Rights Group had begun to help parents articulate demands for better information, more involvement and evidence to justify separation.

A third element was the politically driven concern for accountability in all public services. Children's services had been allowed to expand in a rather uncontrolled way, particularly in response to public and press criticism of notorious failures to protect the victims of abuse. Nevertheless, services could not indefinitely be exempt from the need to monitor standards of performance and demonstrate cost effectiveness. However, such evaluation was impossible without a reliable means of assessing outcome. Each of these pressures, as later chapters show, has become even more compelling in the years since the project was first set up.

The Task of the Working Party

The initial aims and objectives of the original working party were modest. The purpose of their first meeting was to review the current state of knowledge on child care and consider ways of assessing outcomes. An overview of the extensive child care research activity of the early 1980s revealed two important characteristics. Firstly, almost all studies focused on services from the viewpoint of providers and rarely examined the impact of interventions on children or families; moreover, assessments of service outcomes tended to rely on a single measure, such as the breakdown or continuance of placements. Secondly, much research was constrained by administrative boundaries. Because social services carried the responsibility for children in care, areas of importance in a child's life, notably health and education, remained uninvestigated. Provision was seen as being the concern of other agencies (Jackson, 1989; Jackson, 1994; Kahan, 1989).

The evidence presented at that time reinforced misgivings about the quality of the care experience and emphasised the lack of information about its longer term effects. The apparently straightforward question of what happens to children who grow up or spend part of their lives in local authority care simply could not be answered. No adequate measures or assessment instruments existed to assist researchers or practitioners to make judgements about what might be satisfactory or unsatisfactory outcomes. Indeed, on closer examination, the very concept of outcome turned out to be far from straightforward. The consequences for a child of a period in care or accommodation, or a family's experience of social work intervention, are not easily disentangled from the effects of other powerful influences external to social services departments. Furthermore, how can outcomes for children who have spent their whole lives in residential or foster homes be

7

compared with those for young people who have been looked after away from home for a few months? At what point should an outcome be considered to have occurred and how should it be evaluated?

The initial meetings focused on these questions and explored assessment instruments which could be used to collect data on child care outcomes. It was firmly established at an early date that outcome measures must be useful to practitioners as well as to researchers. Although initially many in the working party had the needs of research foremost in mind, as the work progressed they came to see their primary task as the development of a system that would introduce ideas about child care outcomes into social work practice and be effectively used by social workers and carers.

Some of the questions that had to be answered were: What is an outcome in the context of the public care of children? Having defined an outcome, how do we measure it? By what criteria do we evaluate it? When does an outcome occur? Whose perspective do we take? Should we simply be concerned with outcomes for the child, or should we also consider those for the family as a whole? Should we attempt to assess outcomes in relation to the reason why care was provided in the first place or against some general standard of well-being?

The working party took two early decisions: firstly, in line with the well-established principle of children's legislation that the welfare of the child should be the paramount consideration, assessments would focus on outcomes for individual children; secondly, these outcomes would be linked to children's developmental progress, and not simply ask whether the purpose of the intervention had been met. The assessment materials would need to balance long-term and short-term objectives, looking at the overall well-being of the child rather than concentrating on critical events.

It was clear to the working party that if the scheme was to stimulate practice it would need to monitor a child's progress at regular intervals and produce information that would be immediately useful. This meant that the assessment instrument would need to be more ambitious than a series of scores or scales designed only to measure an end-point state (see Parker *et al* (eds), 1991, Chapter Three).

Although standardised scales can be extremely valuable to researchers, they are not necessarily intended as practice tools and often require considerable interpretation before their significance can be appreciated. Moreover, measurements are located within particular professional or disciplinary systems and are easily misunderstood by those outside. A further problem was encountered, namely that on many important aspects of children's development no standardised tests existed.

Thus, the working party set itself the task of designing a comprehensive system in which the relationship between input and outcome would be clearly delineated. In such an approach a negative outcome would not just be taken as a regrettable statement of fact but as a pointer to necessary action; similarly a positive outcome would be not a signal for complacency but a springboard for further progress.

It would be naive to suggest that there is a direct causal relationship between social work interventions, the care provided within placements and outcomes for individual children. Children's lives are profoundly influenced by events over which social services departments have no control. But while it may be impossible to show that a particular long-term outcome for a child resulted directly from social work action, an assessment which adopts an interactionist perspective can determine how far the service offered contributed to the probability of success.

But what is meant by success? What is an appropriate standard by which to judge the care provided for children by public bodies? In the past this was defined as providing for their basic physical needs at a level no better than that experienced by other children from a similar social background. More recently, concern with their emotional experiences has claimed the attention of social workers, especially in Britain and the United States, but this has sometimes been at the expense of attention to more practical matters.

The *Children Act 1989* introduced new standards for child care services, relating them closely to what might be expected of an average parent. Earlier grounds for care and supervision orders were replaced with the question, 'Is the child receiving that care which it would be reasonable to expect a parent to give?' This implies some consensus on what is reasonable parenting and assumes that it will lead to the achievement of a satisfactory quality of life for children. The concept fits well with an interactionist theoretical framework, and with the idea of focusing on intermediate rather than final outcomes in designing any evaluation. This substantially reduces the difficulty of making connections between child care interventions and their effects. The extent to which a child care agency is successfully carrying out its responsibilities can be judged by the extent to which it mirrors the practices of the 'reasonable' parent.

Why do parents do the things they do? In part the answer lies in what Utting (Department of Health, 1991b) has described as 'the selfless character of parental love', which, as he acknowledges, cannot be replaced or replicated. However it is possible to analyse the components of parental behaviour and deduce that it has a sense of direction. Most competent parents have an idea of the outcomes they want for their children and try to encompass them. While this provides a useful starting point, children who come to the attention of public bodies, and especially those who need to be looked after away from home, are likely to have more complex and demanding problems than those growing up with their own families. If they are to recover from the effects of early adverse experiences and achieve outcomes comparable with other children, they may need exceptional support, advice or special treatment.

A Multi-Dimensional View of Child Development

The aim therefore, was to provide a method of assessment that covered all those milestones in growing up which are informally monitored and promoted by 'reasonable' parents. The working party identified seven developmental dimensions along which children need to progress if they are to achieve satisfactory outcomes, defined as 'long-term well-being in adulthood'. These were Health, Education, Identity, Family and Social Relationships, Social Presentation, Emotional and Behavioural Development and Self-Care Skills. Assessment materials were fashioned which not only showed how much progress children were making but also how the care experience contributed to the realisation of their full potential.

These materials comprise six age-related Assessment and Action Records (commonly referred to as the Records) which give a picture of children's day-to-day experiences from birth to adulthood across the seven developmental dimensions. Children are assessed within six age-bands which correspond with the different stages of psycho-social development and are therefore not of equal size; in the original Records these were: under 1, 1–2, 3–4, 5–9, 10–15 and 16+.

Appendix Two shows both the original and the revised education dimension from the Assessment and Action Record for children aged 5–9. As can be seen, the sections begin by specifying what would be the aims of a 'reasonable' parent for a child at that stage of development. Questions then ask whether carers are providing children with those opportunities that are known to maximise achievement. Each leading question triggers a series of subsidiary questions. For example, the original education objectives for 5–9 year-olds were: that the child's educational attainments were average or above, that he or she was acquiring special skills and interests, that he or she was participating fully in school activities and was favourably regarded by teachers. Since we know that school attainment is closely related to reading competence, questions explored what was done to encourage a child to enjoy reading, such as: 'How many books does the child own?' and 'How often does the child go to a library?' If the answers show that the child is not being offered experiences likely to contribute to achieving the objectives, carers are asked to make further plans and decide who will take further action. An explanation is required for gaps in information or decisions to take no remedial action when it appears to be warranted.

Each section of the Records concludes by asking respondents to consult with one another to make joint assessments of outcomes — the extent to which the specified objectives have been achieved. An unsatisfactory assessment should encourage respondents to review earlier questions to see what more might be done. In this way the assessment of deficient outcomes can recommend improvements in practice; on the other hand, good outcomes can provide recognition and reinforcement of good practice. The interaction between outcome, assessment and practice is an important feature of the system and is demonstrated in Figure 1. Each Record ends with a summary sheet designed to encourage respondents to draw together all the plans for further action, to set target dates, allocate responsibilities and monitor the progress of the case.

Three accompanying Planning and Review forms were also published to complement the Assessment and Action Records: a Basic Facts Sheet, a Plan and a Review Form. These demonstrated how the Records could be incorporated into existing arrangements for gathering information, making plans and reviewing children's cases.

Testing the Materials

The report of the working party: *Looking After Children: Assessing Outcomes in Child Care* was generally well received and the preliminary trials of the Assessment and Action Records were sufficiently encouraging for the Department of Health to issue them for use in England and Wales. At that stage, however, the Records had not been tested empirically. What had been established was that the ideas behind the initiative were acceptable to those looking after children away from home and that, if the approach was fully understood, more objective and systematic assessment could follow and lead to better outcomes. It was clear, however, that further testing would be needed if the Assessment and Action Records were to become a routine part of social work practice.

The first study also signalled some of the problems that were likely to be encountered in introducing the materials more

Figure 1

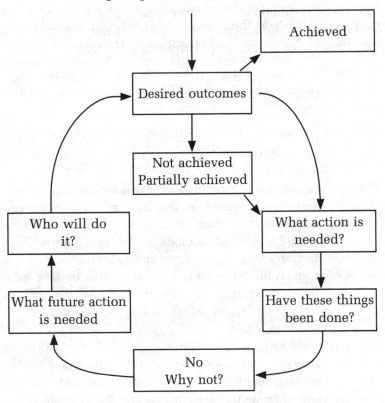

THE MODEL

What do good parents want for their children?

widely. Local authorities had only recently implemented the *Children Act 1989*, and for many the prospect of further innovation was too exhausting to contemplate. (This factor might have diminished with time had not other proposals for changed structures and forms of service delivery appeared almost immediately.) It was also clear from the preliminary trials that social workers were unlikely to use the Assessment and Action Records if they saw them as an additional bureaucratic burden; for implementation to be successful, the Records needed to be perceived as a means of improving practice. A strong policy lead from senior management and close supervision and support were also required. These would need to be combined with effective training and induction if social workers were to understand the principles behind the Records and build them into their practice. The danger was that *Looking After Children* would be seen as an exercise in ticking boxes instead of as a means of improving outcomes.

As a result, the second stage of the work (commonly referred to as the evaluation study), reported in this book, fell into five parts:

1. piloting all the *Looking After Children* materials to see whether they fulfil the functions for which they were designed;
2. ascertaining the views of professionals, carers, parents and children on the content, design and applicability of the materials;
3. a study of implementation in participating local authorities;
4. a study of 204 children looked after in five local authorities designed to discover whether the Records could be used to assess their progress and experiences over time;
5. a study of a community group of 379 children in ordinary families designed to discover whether the content of the Records adequately reflect parents' concerns about the upbringing of their children.

Much of this work has led to modifications of the original approach, and many of the changes reflect priorities other than those of research. In the revised version some of the principles behind the legislation and guidance for children's services, which are of concern to policy makers are more explicitly addressed: for example, the ideal of partnership between social workers, carers and birth families. Much greater attention is given to enabling consumers — children, young people and parents — to express their views and participate in the assessment of outcome. The importance of consulting with significant people outside social services is also given more weight, reflecting an increased awareness of the problems arising from the fragmentation of services.

The views of social workers, foster and residential carers, medical and education advisers and disability specialists have also strongly influenced the final version. Ease of use, ways of saving time and appropriate language (for example, to allow better understanding by young people) had to be taken into account. Finally, a number of administrative questions had to be resolved, such as how *Looking After Children* can be fitted into existing monitoring and review arrangements within social services departments, how often the Assessment and Action Records should be used, who owns them, and how the information that is collected can be fed back to decision makers at policy level.

The compromises and adjustments necessary to meet the concerns of those in the local authorities, the Social Services Inspectorate and the service users have inevitably produced a tool which differs substantially from an academic research instrument. The research team has taken the view, supported by the Social Services Inspectorate, that getting the system into use had to be the first consideration if it were to have any impact on the quality of the care provided.

This part of the study has also explored the various functions of the Assessment and Action Records. For example, they can be used as discussion documents that set out an agenda for interactions between carers, social workers and children and young people. They also act as assessment and planning tools that help practitioners measure children's progress and identify where improvements can be made in the quality of the care they receive. When used alongside the Planning and Review forms, the Records provide a comprehensive system for information-gathering, planning, assessment and review that meets the stringent requirements of the *Children Act 1989*. Finally, as data-collecting instruments, the Assessment and Action Records can gather information about children's experiences which, when aggregated, provides a basis for planning services and directing resources.

As a result of all this activity, the *Looking After Children* materials have been extensively revised and now (1995) contain the following:

Original Version	Revised Version
Basic Facts Sheet	Essential Information Records (Parts One and Two)

Plan	Care Plan
	Placement Plan
	    Part One: Placement Agreement
	    Part Two: Day-to-Day Arrangements

Review Form	Consultation Papers Review Form
Assessment and Action Records	Assessment and Action Records

As the project progressed and interest grew it became clear that if *Looking After Children* were to be implemented across the country, training resources would be needed to introduce managers, social workers and carers to the concepts on which the materials are based and the practical issues that need to be considered before they can be used effectively. It was also clear that a computerised version of the materials would make it easier to store information and analyse data. Both these exercises have now been completed, and the revised *Looking After Children* materials are complemented by a training video, a guide for trainers, practice examples and a reader, a management and implementation guide and a computerised database which replicates the Essential Information Record.

Conclusion

The *Looking After Children* materials aim to improve parenting experiences and outcomes for children looked after by local authorities and other agencies by bringing to the attention of those responsible for their upbringing the probable conse-

16

quences of different actions. In short, they introduce ideas about child care outcomes into social work practice.

The materials set out a number of aims that a reasonable parent might be expected to hold for any child. In so doing, they require those responsible for children's care to consider all aspects of their lives, not only those that have led to a period of separation from home. They also require that plans are made for looked after children and that these are rigorously recorded and acted upon. The materials encourage partnerships between those responsible for a child's care, i.e. between substitute carers, social workers, families and others involved in the child's life. They also promote continuities in the lives of children who are looked after and reduce, indeed wherever possible eliminate, the disruption revealed by much previous child care research.

Used systematically, the materials also benefit the local authority. For example, they form a comprehensive review and monitoring system that meets the requirements of the *Children Act 1989*. As well as providing data that are needed to complete the SSDA 903 return required annually by the Department of Health, the information gathered from the completed materials can be used to produce an aggregate picture of the characteristics of children looked after, the services provided for them and the outcomes of their experiences.

Lest the aims and possible uses of *Looking After Children* appear grandiose, some discussion of the limitations of the system may clarify its special contribution to child care. *Looking After Children* is not a scientifically validated set of instruments which can be used to assess outcomes for children, although the materials draw on the best knowledge available; neither is it a check on the competence of those responsible for children's upbringing, although the materials highlight deficiencies in practice; and, finally, it is not sufficient in itself for the production of information which will allow the performance of local authorities to be contrasted with one another, although experienced researchers will be able to use the data to assess the impact of different combinations of interventions in different need situations.

Given the potential benefits of using *Looking After Children*, we next discuss the ways in which we set about testing and refining the materials.

Chapter 2

Research and Development Strategy 1991–1994

Introduction

At the time of their publication in 1991, the original *Looking After Children* materials had been through preliminary trials, but were still undergoing an extensive programme of evaluation. Initially, the principal aim of this stage of the research (1991–1994) was to assess the viability and relevance of the Assessment and Action Records, the outcome measures devised by the Department of Health working party, which have been universally regarded as the key element of the project. We needed to know what revisions were necessary in order to ensure that the Records adequately address issues which are fundamental to the upbringing and long-term well-being of children looked after away from home; we also needed to assess their usefulness as discussion documents, planning tools and data-gathering instruments and, as a corollary, the likelihood of their being implemented by local authorities for these purposes. By late 1992 it had become apparent that other project materials: the Basic Facts Sheets, the Planning Forms and the Review Forms, had been widely adopted; it was also clear that the successful implementation of the Assessment and Action Records depended on their being used as part of a comprehensive framework for planning and review. The research project was therefore extended in order to evaluate further both the content and the use of these forms.

Evaluating the Assessment and Action Records: The Looked After Group

We originally began to evaluate the Assessment and Action Records by inviting four local authorities each to ask social workers and carers to use them to assess a *looked after study group* of 50 children in care or accommodation. These children were assessed on two occasions, separated by a year. A fifth local authority provided additional assessments when it became apparent that this study group contained an insufficient number of children under the age of five.

The primary purpose of this part of the research was to evaluate the content and usage of the Assessment and Action Records. As we needed to encourage participants to complete the Records, we gave local authorities considerable freedom to choose how the evaluation might best be organised. As a result, Authorities A and B opted to confine the research to a particular area office or team of social workers; in contrast, Authorities C and D chose to assess a scattered cohort of children selected from across each county. Authority E had already decided to adopt the complete *Looking After Children* system to replace their review procedures before we approached them. In this authority, all children who had been looked after for four months or more were, at least in theory, assessed as part of the general reviewing arrangements and they provided 16 cases aged under five, for whom Assessment and Action Records had already been completed, to be included in the looked after group.

These flexible arrangements were designed to discover the circumstances under which the assessments would be most likely to prove useful. Although they have helped to answer the research questions, they have meant that not all children in the looked after group were selected on a random basis. Two of the authorities assessed children whose characteristics were representative of the looked after population as a whole; however, Authority A confined the assessments to young people aged ten or over and Authority C selected a group of children who were experiencing particular difficulties in finding stable placements.

The authorities differed substantially in their geographic and demographic characteristics. Authority A was an urban metropolitan borough, Authorities B and C both had mixed urban and rural populations, one in the South of England, and one in the Midlands. Authority D had a predominantly rural population in the South of England. Authority E was an inner London Borough. We were unfortunate in failing to recruit an authority from the North of England to provide assessments for the looked after group, although three authorities in this region were later identified through the network (see p.26 below) and participated in the evaluation of other *Looking After Children* materials.

Although three of the authorities had substantial populations from African-Caribbean and Asian backgrounds, we had considerable difficulty in identifying children from these groups, largely because respondents preferred not to answer questions concerning ethnicity: indeed, in one authority that participated in later trials of other materials, it was policy not to gather information on this issue. In view of this, it seems likely that, overall, children of mixed race or from minority ethnic groups were under-recorded in the looked after group.

As Chapter Six describes, we initially had some difficulty in finding local authorities that were willing to provide 50 assessments, and in the event we agreed to two authorities producing a reduced quota of 30. However, as Table 2.1 demonstrates, although one authority failed to complete the agreed number of assessments, two others produced substantially more than expected within the required timescale.

With the inclusion of the assessments from Authority E, the complete looked after group contained 204 children of whom 121 (59%) were assessed once and 83 (41%) twice. The lower rate for second assessments arose because the children had returned home or moved to another area and reviewing procedures had ceased or been transferred. In only a very few cases was the failure to repeat assessments due to lack of time

Table 2.1: *Assessments Produced by Participating Authorities*

Authority	Assessments Promised	Assessments Produced
A	30	30
B	50	63
C	30	57
D	50	38
Subtotal	**160**	**188**
E	Not applicable	16
Total		**204**

or insufficient commitment. Nevertheless this finding was one of the first indications that a concerted effort would be needed if the Assessment and Action Records were to be used effectively and on a regular basis for all children in care or accommodation.

Social workers were primarily responsible for ensuring that the Assessment and Action Records were completed, although much of the work was undertaken by carers and by young people themselves. The researchers visited the authorities at regular intervals and invited participants to answer question-naires and produce oral and written comments in addition to completing the Records.

The Community Group

From an early stage we were concerned that the results from the evaluation study as it was originally conceived would not be able to resolve a key issue raised by participants and others who had read about the work. The original Assessment and Action Records had been designed in the abstract by a group of academics and practitioners and then briefly trialed by social workers, carers, parents and children and young people before publication. The Records ask statutory agencies to assess whether carers are offering children the opportunities for growth and development that we would expect good parents to provide as a matter of course, and in doing so, they claim to reflect the concerns that ordinary parents have about their children. Yet we have very little objective information about what parents actually do. The Newsons' longitudinal study (1963, 1968, 1976) asks different questions from those we were posing, and some of their earlier material is now out of date. The recent ESRC programme of research on the experiences of young men and women moving from adolescence to adulthood is restricted to a limited age-group, and does not cover all the issues we wanted to address (Banks *et al*, 1992). In order to substantiate our claim that the Assessment and Action Records do indeed reflect the concerns and practices of ordinary parents, we decided to use the materials to assess a *community group* of children who were *not* looked after by child care agencies.

One of the key principles of *Looking After Children* is that parenting is a process that is shared between individuals and the community: we needed to be sure that our community group would have access to the same education, health and leisure services as our looked after group. Children in the community group were therefore drawn from two of the local authorities (A and B) that were already assessing children for the looked after group and, indeed, from localities within these authorities where the social services area team was using the Records to assess all or most of their looked after children. One was an inner city area, and the other an area with mixed rural and semi-industrial characteristics.

The looked after group was identified in order to evaluate the content and potential usage of the Assessment and Action Records and not primarily to provide a profile of children in care or accommodation; similarly, the fundamental purpose of selecting the community group was not to collect information about children in the community living with their families, but to establish how far the issues dealt with by the Records were regarded by ordinary parents as a necessary part of their task.

Restrictions in the timetable and the resources available led to a decision to aim for a group of children who would be concentrated in four age-groups, each covered by a separate Assessment and Action Record. We aimed for a community group of 400 children, and were successful in gathering data on 100 children approaching school age; 89 in school year four (8–9 year-olds), 101 in school year eight (12–13 year-olds), and 89 who had just passed school leaving age (16–17 year olds). In this way we hoped to assess a sufficient number of children in particular age-groups to draw meaningful conclusions from the data.

Selection was undertaken by contacting representative secondary and infant schools in each of the participating areas. We were already aware that the Assessment and Action Records would need to be modified for use with children with physical disabilities or special educational needs, and we therefore decided not to interview children attending special schools. Schools that were willing to participate subsequently contacted all parents of children in particular age ranges on our behalf; we were able to offer a modest fee to any family that agreed to take part. We then approached a random selection of those pupils whose parents had agreed to their being interviewed. Nurseries, colleges of further education and the careers service were also instrumental in enabling us to obtain access to younger children and those over 16 who were in full-time, part-time or day release further education, as well as young people in work or who were unemployed. Snowballing techniques were also used, particularly for children and young people under five or over 16, in order to try to broaden the group to include those not in nursery, further education or known to the careers service. However, the group did not include children from private schools.

Overall response rates were very good, and a high proportion of parents and children from a wide range of socio-economic groups agreed to participate after the aims of the research had been explained. However, in spite of our being able to pay an interview fee, we found that in some of the more deprived districts, substantially fewer families were willing to participate than in other areas. We can only speculate about the reasons for this, although it could be argued that it was the most dysfunctional families, whose children were most likely to have similarities to those being cared for by a public agency, who were the least willing to be interviewed. If this is true, it may be that the resulting data are biased in favour of the more functional families in the community.

A questionnaire, which aimed to collect demographic details as well as additional information regarding family composition, periods of separation and the number of home and school changes, was filled in with each family prior to the completion of the Assessment and Action Record. We were particularly interested to discover whether social class, family income, frequent changes of address or the separation or remarriage of parents affected responses to the Records. We also collected information on the extent to which families displayed characteristics identified by Bebbington and Miles (1989) as increasing the probability of a child's being looked after by a local authority. By this method we were able to identify a group of children with characteristics similar to those looked after, although the numbers were too small for a robust comparison to be made.

Most of the interviews were conducted in the homes of children and young people, although many of those over 16 took up the option to be interviewed on their own, for example in a room supplied by a local college. Our aim was to replicate the use of the Assessment and Action Records in social services departments by completing them in partnership with parents and children and using them to facilitate discussion of specific parenting issues. However, our relationship with children and parents was necessarily different from that of a social worker or carer; with some families the interviewers were unable to establish sufficient rapport in the time allowed to ask some of the more personal questions. We were also unable to involve other interested parties such as teachers and health visitors, as should happen when the Records are completed with looked after children.

We found that children approaching school age played a minimal but important part in the proceedings and often enjoyed drawing pictures or showing how they could write the letters of their names, whilst eight-year-olds were initially fascinated, but lost interest about half way through. Twelve-year-olds, however, took a substantial part, with occasional input from parents, whilst many of those aged over 16 were interviewed individually. The length of the interviews varied, but on average they took between one and a half and two hours.

The information from this community group was used to examine how far the content of the Assessment and Action Records reflects parental practices that are widely accepted as both important and necessary. In addition to completion of an Assessment and Action Record and a questionnaire, feedback was also sought from parents, children and young people about the content, order and style of the materials and their comments were subsequently taken into account during revisions.

The Network of Users

The previous discussion explains how the research project was able to draw on formal data collected from two sources: *the looked after group* and *the community group*. However, as the first edition of the *Looking After Children* materials had been published in 1991, at the beginning of the major phase of the research, a number of organisations which were not formally taking part in their evaluation began to use them as a regular part of social work practice. In addition to the formal data collection, the project also benefited from extensive feedback from practitioners, carers and young people who were using the materials outside the research setting but were anxious to contribute to their development. In 1993 we set up a *network of users* both within and outside the research authorities. It was through this network that we were able to identify authorities that were undertaking their own evaluations of the research materials; representatives from some of these authorities were then invited to collaborate with the research team in providing formal feedback on the revisions to the Assessment and Action Records and other project materials, in piloting training materials and in advising us about computerisation. By the conclusion of the project, 11 local authorities had taken part in formal pilot studies, and we were in close consultation with representatives from a large number of others; two representatives from local authorities were seconded to the research team for the final 18 months of the project's lifetime.

Collaborative Work with Local Authorities: The Planning and Review Forms

In 1993 we became aware through this network that the Planning and Review forms (the Basic Facts Sheet, the Plans and the Review Forms) were being used extensively. These forms had been produced in order to demonstrate how the Assessment and Action Records might fit into existing information-gathering and reviewing structures, but had never been tested in the field. A number of local authorities had begun to use them without introducing the Assessment and Action Records, as though they were the Department of Health recommended planning and review procedures; however the forms were not designed to stand alone and authorities had inevitably come across a number of anomalies. It was also becoming apparent that the Assessment and Action Records needed to be set within a well-constructed reviewing and monitoring system if they were to be used to advantage (see Chapter Six). We therefore set up a working party of representatives from five local authorities who undertook to revise, develop, and pilot these forms. Because it was felt that the original versions needed such considerable revisions that their continued use would be a deterrent to the implementation of the Assessment and Action Records, a revised, interim edition was published in February, 1994. All the five authorities represented on the working party then implemented this edition for all their looked after children and gathered feedback from users, which served as the basis for the production of the more definitive version published in 1995.

Although this initiative was originally led by the research team, in its later stages the working party was chaired and organised by local authority personnel, with the researchers and the Social Services Inspectorate taking a consultative role.

Collaborative Work with Local Authorities: Children with Disabilities

Early responses from social workers assessing children for the looked after group and feedback from the network of users also indicated that the original materials did not adequately cover the circumstances of children with disabilities. In 1993, we set up another working party whose brief was to explore these issues further. Although it was co-ordinated by a researcher with a special interest in children with disabilities, this group consisted largely of representatives from local authorities, one of whom took the chair. Working in close consultation with the Council for Disabled Children and with representatives from the major children's voluntary organisations, this group first devised a set of supplementary questions designed to explore further issues of particular concern to children with disabilities. This supplementary section was then piloted, alongside the revised Assessment and Action Records, with children with disabilities in the five local authorities represented on the working party. Two other local authorities piloted the revised Records, including the supplementary section, with a cross section of all their children. A major aim of this particular trial was to ensure that the revised materials gave sufficient weight to issues of concern to all children, both the able-bodied and the disabled, and did not show an undue bias towards the needs of either group.

Additional Collaboration with Other Agencies

The *Looking After Children* materials were designed to assess and monitor the quality and effectiveness of parenting as it is undertaken by public agencies. Neither social workers nor parents act in isolation, and there are times when they need to co-ordinate their activities with those of other parties who have a particular interest in children's welfare, such as teachers and health professionals. It became apparent at a fairly early stage that professionals outside social services departments sometimes viewed the materials as an inducement to social workers to overstep their role. This issue would become particularly prominent if the materials were widely used and were seen to conflict with other standardised monitoring instruments employed by, for instance, education or health authorities. In order to eradicate such anomalies, two consultation groups drawn from health and education professionals with a particular interest in looked after children gave specific advice on the content of the revised Records.

The Bulletin

Finally, as interest in the project developed, it became clear that we needed to provide an effective channel of communication between the research team, policy makers, practitioners and all other parties involved in the consultation process. We did this by means of a *bulletin* written by the research team in collaboration with practitioners and policy makers, and sent free to anybody who had expressed an interest in being kept up to date with new developments. The bulletin was also distributed to all directors of social services, all social work courses, and to key policy makers who were not directly involved in the project. By the end of the research there were well over a thousand people on the mailing list. The bulletin was seen to be useful not only in developing the materials and extending them beyond the confines of the original research, but also in implementing them successfully.

Collaborative Work with Policy Makers

The initial purpose of the evaluation project was to produce refined and revised versions of the Assessment and Action Records that had been thoroughly tested in the field. Although our aim was always to provide materials that would enable local authorities to make regular assessments of the quality of the service they were providing to looked after children, we did not at first envisage that they would be used more widely than as a specific research or inspection exercise. It was not until a number of authorities (including two that were assessing children for the looked after group) incorporated the materials into departmental policy that we began to examine the issues surrounding implementation. As this issue came to the fore it became necessary for the researchers to work closely not only with representatives from local authorities, but also with policy makers, and the later stages of the project were undertaken in close collaboration with members of the Social Services Inspectorate.

This collaboration proved to be useful to all parties, and was undoubtedly necessary to the development of the project. However, it was not an easy process, for each side had its own agenda. Although all parties were genuinely interested in developing a means of assessment that had obvious advantages for looked after children, they were also driven by other concerns which did not necessarily coincide: the representatives from the local authorities, for instance, needed to ensure that the materials would not prove unnecessarily burdensome to their staff and would be valued as a means of stimulating discussion rather than be disparaged as yet another bureaucratic exercise. Once policy makers had agreed on the value of the materials, agencies needed to be given sufficient encouragement to use them without this being perceived as unnecessary interference from central government. Policy makers also needed to be certain that the revised version reflected both the letter and the spirit of the legislation. The incorporation of the materials into the official series on the *Children Act 1989* from the time of their first publication meant that even the original version was perceived by users as a government approved standard. This being the case, it became clear that all subsequent revisions would need to be undertaken in close consultation with policy makers.

The research team acted as the bridge between practitioners and policy makers; its role was to render the research messages accessible through tried and tested materials that were acceptable to both parties. Evaluating the development and implementation of these materials was also part of the brief. This was not an easy role to play. Firstly, the development of the materials beyond the theoretical stage depended on constructive criticism from practitioners: not all the criticism was constructive and, as we shall see, some of it came from parties with strong moral or ideological views which had little relevance to the project. Several members of the team had been involved in the production of the original version of the materials; they found it difficult not to retain a somewhat proprietorial interest in them. We had to learn to accept and take notice of valid criticism rather than to respond defensively.

Secondly, although we were involved in some of the dissemination that accompanied the policy makers' initiative to encourage implementation, researchers need to retain a degree of independence. We found this extremely difficult to sustain. It is very gratifying to see a project grow from a small beginning to become a major initiative; and yet our role was not to promote the use of the materials, but to discover how helpful they were, and how, and in what contexts they might be used effectively. Issues concerning the dissemination of research messages need to be examined as dispassionately as the original projects, and will be considered as an integral part of this report.

Thirdly, the discussions with practitioners identified further needs which had to be met if the implementation of *Looking After Children* was to be successful. Eighteen months into the project it was decided to develop training materials for practitioners and a system for computerising data.

Conclusion

It should be clear that this research had several functions. Its main purpose was to evaluate a series of practical outcome measures: the Assessment and Action Records. These were designed to provide a means of assessing the consequences of social workers' interventions with children. The procedures do this by asking how far children looked after by public authorities receive the type of care which it would be reasonable to expect a parent to provide, on the assumption that satisfactory progress will usually be linked to the quality of care which children receive. A key question in the evaluation study was to discover how far those parental practices identified by researchers as necessary to the achievement of successful outcomes reflect a popular consensus, and how far public parenting matches the pattern to be found in private families. Thus, this evaluation was undertaken not only to assess the content of the materials, but also to discover whether, when used by local authorities, they fulfilled the functions for which they were designed. The following chapters describe both how the research findings informed the alterations to the materials and how they were used to identify their strengths and weaknesses as discussion tools, as planning documents and as data-gathering instruments.

Two questions remain which cannot be fully answered until data are gathered over a lengthy period: does using the Assessment and Action Records improve the quality of care which children receive, and do improvements in the quality of care, in fact as well as in theory, affect long-term outcomes for looked after children?

Summary Points

1. The purpose of the second stage evaluation study was to discover what revisions were needed to ensure that the Assessment and Action Records reflected issues of genuine importance to the upbringing and well-being of children looked after away from home. We also needed to assess their value as discussion documents, planning tools and research instruments.

2. Social workers in five local authorities provided completed assessments for 204 children. In order to

discover the circumstances under which the Records might prove most useful, authorities were free to choose how they would select the looked after group: some assessed all children who were the responsibility of a particular area office or team, while others chose to select children from across a wider area. Some authorities used the Records as a free-standing assessment exercise, while others used them as part of their reviewing and planning system. Initial fears that we would have difficulty in reaching the target number proved to be unfounded.

3. In order to test our claim that the Assessment and Action Records reflected the concerns and practices of ordinary parents, we also used them to assess a randomly selected community group of 379 children who were not looked after by social services departments. The children came from the same geographical areas as those in the looked after group and were identified with the assistance of the education authority and the careers service. Children and young people were interviewed with their parents in their own homes; some older teenagers took up the option to be assessed on their own, at a neutral venue.

4. Working parties were established to revise and pilot the Planning and Review forms and to examine how the Assessment and Action Records might be adapted to give better attention to issues of concern for children with disabilities. Consultation groups of health and education professionals advised us on specific issues and on revisions that would promote partnerships between social services and other agencies.

5. The project relied on close collaboration between researchers, practitioners and policy makers. Communication between all the parties involved in the formal research exercise, the advisory groups and

the large network of practitioners now using the project materials as part of their everyday work with children was facilitated by means of the publication of a regular bulletin which was sent free of charge to all interested parties.

6. As the project progressed, further needs emerged which had to be met if the implementation of *Looking After Children* was to be successful. Plans were made to develop training materials and a computer programme.

Part Two

Developing the Assessment and Action Records as discussion documents

Chapter 3

Meeting the Content of the Assessment
and Action Records

Part Two

Developing the Assessment and Action Records as Measured Documents

Chapter 3

Revising the content of the Assessment and Action Records

Introduction

The Assessment and Action Records were originally designed as research instruments that might enable local authorities to assess the consequences of social work interventions with children. The Records were intended to produce quantifiable and comparable data of value to researchers in both academic and local authority settings. They aimed to gather objective information about how children and young people develop across seven dimensions: health, education, identity, family and social relationships, social presentation, emotional and behavioural development and self care skills. Within each dimension questions asked how far children were receiving the type of opportunities that both research and experience had identified as necessary to the achievement of satisfactory outcomes; those responsible for children's welfare (including carers and young people themselves) were then required to make joint assessments of their progress towards specific objectives, in consultation with one another.

Although the original intention of the working party was to produce research instruments, it became apparent that the methodology had considerable potential to improve child care practice and consequently outcomes. The issue of developing materials that might enable practitioners to engage more effectively with children and young people in care or accommodation began to take precedence over the question of whether such instruments might collect valid and reliable data. In fact, during the course of the project we were advised to alter our focus: in 1992 the Department of Health and participating agencies decided that widespread use of the Records would give looked after children better opportunities to achieve satisfactory outcomes and that local authorities should be encouraged to implement them as a regular part of social work practice; from then on we were asked to develop the materials as practice tools rather than as research instruments. The subsequent emphasis has been on designing tools which direct practitioners towards those issues which research has shown to influence children's progress. The problems of implementation thus became an increasingly pressing concern.

The Records continue to produce data which can be of great value to researchers and are being used for this purpose either in a complete or an abbreviated form in a large number of research projects both in Britain and abroad. However, the work of identifying those questions which will provide local authorities with useful information about outcomes for groups of children for whom they are responsible and ensuring that responses from practitioners are both accurate and reliable has still to be undertaken. Funding has been agreed to examine the validity of the responses to the questions on emotional and behavioural development (see pp. 42–45 below) and there are also plans to undertake similar work on other parts of the Records, including the assessments of objectives. The advantage of developing the materials initially as practice tools and validating them later is that we know from this stage of the research that they are acceptable to the practitioners who will be asked to use them.

The Format of the Original Records

The original working party on child care outcomes had come to the conclusion that parents monitor their children's growth and development across the seven dimensions already noted and that progress along all of these appears to be necessary to healthy development. Obviously, some parents will have higher specific aspirations for their children than others, but there are certain baseline goals within each dimension which all reasonable parents hold in common. Disagreements are most likely to occur over the most appropriate routes by which these goals may be achieved and over which reasons are acceptable for not taking recommended actions. The Assessment and Action Records are intended to reflect this universality of intention and to indicate those routes which research has shown to be the most likely to lead to success. In theory the Records could be used to assess outcomes for all children, although they give additional emphasis to issues that are known to be of particular significance to those looked after by the state.

The Assessment and Action Records all have a similar format. As was explained in the introduction, children and young people are divided into six age-groups. Within each age-group assessments are made across seven developmental dimensions. As Appendix Two demonstrates, in each dimension the Record begins by setting out what objectives a reasonable parent might hold for a child of that age, in that particular area. Respondents are then asked a number of questions designed to find out whether the child is receiving care of a sufficiently high standard to enable him or her to reach these objectives. At the end of each dimension, all respondents are asked to make a joint assessment of how far the child has progressed towards achieving the objectives already described.

On the original Records, questions for children and young people up to the age of 15 were addressed to their carers; those for young people aged 16 and over were addressed to them directly. The accompanying booklet of guidelines advised that, while it was the social worker's responsibility to ensure that the work was undertaken, parents, carers, health visitors and teachers might often be in a better position to provide answers to the questions they cover. In fact, the task of completing the Records was and still is, envisaged as a joint exercise to be undertaken by all those who share responsibility for a child's progress, in consultation with one another. All children and young people of sufficient age and understanding were encouraged to participate in this exercise, although they were not expected to complete the Records by themselves, even when the questions were addressed directly to them.

Revisions

The content of the materials was evaluated by means of a critical appraisal of completed Assessment and Action Records from two study groups: the 204 children looked after in five local authorities and the 379 parents and children interviewed in the community group. Information also came from responses to questionnaires that had been designed to elicit comments from social workers, carers and children and young people using the Records either as part of the research or as part of social work practice. Responses to role-play exercises that were undertaken as part of the formal national dissemination organised by the Social Services Inspectorate provided a further source of critical information.

Age-groupings
The six age-specific Assessment and Action Records were designed to correspond to different stages in a child's psychosocial development. The first three age-groups (under 1, 1–2 and 3–4) covered the stages of development in the pre-school years; 5-9 years encompassed the years of middle childhood spent at primary and junior school, 10–15 years covered the transition to secondary school and the onset of adolescence. The last, open-ended, age-band, 16 years and over, dealt with issues concerning the approach of independence. The age-groups were of uneven size because more rapid changes occur in early childhood than in later years (Parker *et al*, 1991). The groupings were generally considered acceptable although respondents found that the questions on the 10–15 year-old Record covered too great a developmental span. Fifteen-year-olds generally found the Record for older teenagers (16+) covered issues that were more closely related to their development and experience and so we lowered the cut-off point for this age-group by one year.

40

We also followed advice to lower the age at which questions were addressed directly to children and young people. Under the *Children Act 1989*, local authorities now have a duty to ascertain the wishes and feelings of children they look after before making any decisions about them (S.22.3). Asking children and young people about their welfare directly encourages them to participate fully in the assessment and reminds adults to ensure that they are involved in decision-making. We did, however, encounter considerable tension between those who believe that children should be consulted and involved in decisions and those who think that this should be taken further and feel strongly that they should be encouraged to make important decisions about their future themselves. If children and young people are to grow towards independence, they need to be given sufficient autonomy to feel that they are in control of their lives; yet one of the most difficult parental tasks is to learn when and in what areas to delegate responsibility. Data from both the looked after and community groups showed that parents and carers regularly offered the child's wishes as a reason for deciding not to pursue courses of action which might otherwise have been regarded as beneficial. Although one could argue that these were laudable examples of how children's views are now being taken seriously, we should point out that we found four-year-olds who had decided not to go to the dentist and 14-year-olds whose decision to smoke was regarded as acceptable. While it is obviously damaging to exclude children and young people from discussions about their lives, it can be equally disadvantageous to encourage them to make decisions that will radically affect their future before they are equipped to weigh up the advantages and disadvantages. Children's wishes do not always coincide with their own best interests and at times it seemed as though parents and carers were promoting their need for self-determination in order to hide their own lack of authority.

This issue not only encompassed the practical question of determining when children are sufficiently mature to make autonomous decisions that will have long-term and possibly unlooked-for consequences, but also the ethical debate about children's rights. We constantly found that the need for an open debate over this and other concerns was obscured by ideological pressures.

Dimensions

Responses from parents and children in the community group confirmed that the seven developmental dimensions identified by the working party are indeed the areas in which they informally monitor children's progress. The only issue that they did not consider to be adequately covered by the Records was discipline—a cause of tension in all families, whatever their circumstances. Although many parents considered that this was such an important issue that it needed to be considered in a separate section, we felt that the negotiation of rules and sanctions should not be treated as a new dimension, but should be given greater prominence in the section concerning children's emotional and behavioural development and have amended the Records accordingly. Apart from this criticism about the structure of the Records, almost all the comments on content concerned the questions about parental practices and tended to fall into one of three categories: academic, ideological and pragmatic.

Academic Issues: Emotional and Behavioural Development and Family and Social Relationships

After selecting the dimensions, the original working party had devoted considerable attention to the question of how development in these areas might be assessed. One obvious solution was to invite local authorities to assess children's progress using existing measures with known psychometric properties. However, it was clearly not possible to assemble a package of such instruments that covered the right topics and age ranges and that was short and simple enough to be used by staff who had no specialist training for the purpose. Moreover, there was considerable concern that while the regular administration of detailed psychometric tests might eventually enable local authorities to map children's progress, the exercise could easily ignore questions of accountability. If assessment concentrated on end results, it would always be possible to excuse lack of progress by citing the trauma many looked after children had experienced in early life; yet there was increasing evidence that the care services frequently failed to provide the compensatory experiences disadvantaged children need in order to achieve their potential. The Assessment and Action Records were designed to address these difficulties: they not only ask respondents to provide assessments of children's progress, they also seek to establish whether those looked after are being offered the type of experiences that are necessary to success.

Although the Assessment and Action Records are not yet validated, they are nevertheless firmly rooted in research. The questions about children's experiences are based on the best evidence we have so far about effective parental actions; practitioners and carers are given this information in a series of relatively simple questions and then invited to act on it. Responses from parents and children in the community group suggested that much of this information is already recognised as being fundamental to the upbringing of children.

While most of these recommended parental actions are of proven importance, such as the provision of a nutritious diet, the importance of others remains to be more firmly established. In revising the Records we have replaced some untested material with validated measures, and plan to validate those sections that are, as yet, untried, a process that will continue as knowledge of effective parenting increases.

The major changes of this nature have been on the emotional and behavioural development sections. It is well known that many looked after children have severe emotional and behavioural difficulties. These can provide some of the most troublesome problems for carers and, if they are not dealt with, can affect the lives of children and young people into adulthood. Therefore, where such problems exist, interventions must try to provide an environment where they can be addressed. In order to identify possible difficulties, carers and young people are asked to make ratings on behaviours and feelings that cause them concern.

The original items in the list were based on research evidence about problematic behaviours and feelings that need to be dealt with if children are to develop satisfactorily towards adulthood (e.g. Hoghughi, 1978). However, in the evaluation of the Records, three shortcomings were highlighted. Firstly, the rating approach proved problematic. Carers and social workers were asked to indicate where children fell on a particular item by making a mark on a continuous line bounded by two extremes. This system of recording was found to be confusing to use and would have made it difficult to compare children with one another or across time. Secondly, feedback from researchers argued that the sections would be improved if the items were expanded to allow their grouping into sub-scales that measured problems in line with current clinical diagnostic thinking. Thirdly, it was felt by carers and researchers that there was insufficient emphasis on strengths and too much on difficulties. For these reasons the section has been expanded to cover a wider range of items, to make the wording more acceptable to users, to include more positive features of behaviour and to cover the main dimensions of problems in feelings and behaviour identified by clinical practice and research (see Rutter and Rutter, 1994; Rutter, Taylor and Hersov, 1994).

The approach taken in redrafting these sections has been to cover the same broad areas of feelings and behaviour, but appropriately tailored to each age group. This will make it easier to track changes in these areas over time. The new sections are based on existing instruments that are known to distinguish children with significant emotional and behavioural problems reliably from those without — the Rutter A scale and its modifications (Goodman, 1994; Rutter, Tizard and Whitmore, 1970). However, in order to meet the concerns of practitioners the rating scheme has been modified. In the Rutter and Goodman scales carers are asked to indicate for each item, whether 'it definitely applies', 'applies somewhat' or 'doesn't apply' to the child. The new scales on the Assessment and

Action Records ask carers to say how like the child or young person are the descriptions of behaviours or feelings contained in these items. Older children and young people are also asked to give independent ratings that can be compared with those made by carers. Four point ratings are used; for example the young person is asked to say whether the behaviour described is 'definitely like me', 'quite like me', 'a bit like me' or 'not at all like me'. This change in format means that the instruments and their sub-scales need to be re-validated in order to make sure the individual dimensions (sub-scales) identified in the Rutter scales are reproduced satisfactorily and to establish the cutting points that suggest more serious problems.

The sections contain a number of individual items, each of which might indicate a problem or concern to which someone ought to pay attention, even in isolation. However, in line with the normal use of such instruments, problems only become of clinical significance when a child scores on a number of items. The patterning of the items indicates a particular type of problem, for example, emotional or conduct problems, over-activity and restlessness, or difficulties in social relationships. It cannot be emphasised too strongly that instruments of this kind do not provide a clinical diagnosis of children's problems: their purpose is to help identify, or 'screen' for those children or young people whose difficulties may need a more systematic specialist assessment.

An attempt to introduce additional validated material into the dimension of family and social relationships encountered greater difficulties. The Dartington study on children's return home from care or accommodation (Bullock et al, 1993) has produced a series of checklists that indicate to professionals the likelihood of a separated child being returned to relatives and the chances of any such reunion being successful. We considered the possibility of introducing these checklists into the Records. However, while the return study was designed to assess the progress of children looked after and to predict their living situations, the Assessment and Action Records were concerned with other aspects of family and social relationships and were designed to be used with all children, including those living at home. We had, therefore, to be satisfied with including information from the return study in the Planning and Review forms described in Chapter Six.

Ideological Issues: Identity and Education

In common with the parents in the community group, social workers and carers assessing children and young people for the looked after group or in the normal course of their duties found that most of the questions were acceptable, although they were generally doubtful about the extent to which the materials addressed the needs of children with disabilities, an issue that will be considered later in this chapter. However, they tended to be much more concerned than were parents with a number of ideological questions.

We have already seen how the debate about children's rights affected the manner in which the questions were drafted. Over the course of the study we also found ourselves grappling with issues concerning the rights of minority ethnic groups, children with disabilities and gay and lesbian adolescents. We also encountered many different perceptions of working class culture. Social workers act as advocates for the disadvantaged and it is inevitable that, in the present climate, they should become enmeshed in the debate about political correctness. Although it was obviously our task to ensure that the content of the Assessment and Action Records contained nothing which might unwittingly cause offence, as researchers we needed to retain a degree of objectivity in the face of what were often considerable pressures to adopt a particular ideological stance.

Identity
It had been difficult to obtain comments from representatives of minority ethnic groups before the original Assessment and Action Records were published and there was some concern that the materials might be perceived as possessing too strong a bias towards the white majority culture. After publication, feedback from some authorities did indeed suggest that the

questions on identity gave insufficient attention to the situation of black children and we amended the Records to give greater prominence to questions concerning race, language, religion and culture. We also altered the language throughout the Records to reflect more closely the nature of the multi-cultural society in which many children live: for instance we have now included examples of Muslim religious festivals and foods traditionally eaten by the African-Caribbean population in questions about holidays and diet. Responses from some of the shire counties, in contrast, where the majority culture is still largely unaffected by immigration, sometimes expressed the opposite concern, that the Records gave too great a prominence to issues which were largely inapplicable to their care population. The Records are intended as a means of assessing the experiences and progress of children on a national basis: their success as a practice tool will depend on their ability to address the needs of a wide range of children without giving undue prominence to those of any particular group: the task of steering a course between a number of legitimate but conflicting interests was not easy.

Although we found it necessary to make these changes, we were somewhat concerned by the finding that a number of respondents assumed that the questions on identity were only relevant to black or mixed race children. This is, of course, a misconception. The establishment of a secure sense of self is fundamental to the development of any child, whatever their race or culture. Children from minority cultures may have particular issues to confront in this area, but by no means all of them will be concerned with race: a sense of identity is also developed through the knowledge that one belongs to a particular religious, cultural, social and linguistic group, as well as, most importantly, to a particular family.

Scottish, Irish or European children living in England, the children of travellers, those whose families belong to unusual religious sects or whose lifestyle does not match a stereotype, all will need to reinforce a sense of identity that may be threatened or discriminated against by the majority. Moreover, while children from minority groups may have specific developmental tasks to undertake in this area, there are other aspects of identity which have no ideological or racial overtones. The identity dimension includes a number of questions designed to discover, for instance, whether carers are encouraging children and young people to develop a sense of self-worth and direction in their lives and an understanding of their family background and past history.

The view that the questions on identity would only cover racial issues was commonly held by white parents and children in the community group, who tended to ignore these questions, but it was not unusual to find such assumptions also among social workers and carers. Parents are rarely trained in child development and they may well only verbalise the need to ensure that their children develop a secure sense of identity if there are clearly recognised obstacles, such as membership of a group which experiences discrimination. However, trained social workers regularly face these issues and could be more aware of their significance. Research on adoption, for instance, has shown that children who no longer live with birth parents encounter difficulties in acquiring a sense of belonging even when they are in secure, successful placements (Triseliotis and Russell, 1984); looked after children may also have difficulties in coming to terms with their past history and their present situation and with integrating their experiences into a positive self-image. Being looked after by a local authority is in itself a stigmatising experience and all children in this situation need to know how to deal with the discrimination that is likely to ensue. Yet social workers sometimes adopted similar views to parents and occasionally ignored the questions on identity if the child were white. That there is a need for further training in this area is demonstrated by the responses on completed Records. We found that one in eight of the 10–15 year olds in the looked after group were unable to explain why they were not living with their parents; of those who could explain, more than one in three had received no help in deciding what to say when people asked probing questions about their family background or care situation. One 11-year-old had been in care for seven years in eight different placements; she was unable to say why she was looked after by the local authority and told enquirers: 'I just say I live with Mum and Dad'.

Education

While the questions on identity raised a number of overtly political issues, particularly among white parents in the community group who sometimes used them as an opportunity to express racial prejudices, it was those on education which social workers found the most controversial. Some argued that the Records promoted middle class values that have little relevance to looked after children. Some questions, such as the one asking how well a child was doing at school or whether he or she had achieved the aim of producing educational attainments that were average or above, were insensitively phrased, particularly for children with learning difficulties, and the revised version seeks to avoid this. However, much of the criticism was aimed at the recommended parental actions. The question that caused most controversy was repeated on all the Records for children from 4–15 years and asked about access to books and libraries. Other questions that attracted similar criticism were one on the 5–9-year-old Record which asked whether children were learning to play musical instruments and another that asked 10–15 year-olds if they had a quiet place to do their homework.

These criticisms came exclusively from respondents who assessed children in the looked after group or engaged in a critical appraisal of the materials as part of the dissemination exercise, and were not voiced by parents and children in the community group. Only 9% of children in the community group had limited access to books: even in these families, parents regarded this as a genuine issue, although they did not always have the wherewithal to engineer a change: it was only the children in the looked after group whose carers thought the question irrelevant. There is a wealth of research that demonstrates the link between encouragement to read at home and educational achievement (Tizard *et al*, 1982; Tizard *et al*, 1988; Osborn and Milbank, 1987); there is also evidence that looked after children frequently lag behind their peers in literacy skills (Garnett, 1994; Department for Education, 1994; Fletcher-Campbell and Hall, 1990). It is therefore disappointing to find that some of those who share parental responsibility for such children dismiss the suggestion that they might need to be encouraged to read on the grounds that this reflects unrealistic aspirations. The recent study by the *Who Cares?* magazine, in which selected looked after children were offered grants to spend on books, was also criticised for attempting to foster inappropriate middle class aspirations amongst deprived children (Bald and Bean, forthcoming). In some quarters there is an assumption that it is somehow inappropriate, and indeed unfair, to encourage looked after children to succeed academically. Such attitudes probably lie behind the lack of attention given to the education of children in care or accommodation. Neither *Looking After Children* nor *Who Cares?* make ambitious assumptions about children's academic abilities: they have simply been criticised for promoting the view that literacy skills are important.

The question about whether looked after children were learning to play musical instruments also attracted the criticism that it reflected a middle class aspiration that was irrelevant to the families of children in care or accommodation. The evidence from our data demonstrates the fallacy of this assumption: in the 5–9 year-old age-group a third of the looked after children and nearly half of those from all social classes in the community group were learning to play musical instruments. While middle class children will be more likely to have private piano lessons, it is wrong to assume that music is their prerogative. The likelihood of children in the community group learning to play instruments was more dependent on the adequacy of the local school music service than on social class.

We did not alter the Records in response to these criticisms because we concluded that they derived from an ideology which was essentially detrimental to the welfare of the children concerned. The assumption that only middle class parents will encourage their children to read or to enjoy music is belied by the evidence from our data and serves only to depress expectations for looked after children. Those who adopt this position generally do so from a genuine desire to avoid making unnecessary judgements; yet to assume that the parents of looked after children have lower aspirations for them than do other parents is a judgement in itself and one that does nothing to improve their situation.

Pragmatic Issues About Relevance: All Dimensions

While the questions on emotional and behavioural development have been altered to take account of particular academic issues and those on identity and education have been influenced but not, we hope, unduly swayed by a number of ideological considerations, the content of all the dimensions has been revised in order to make them more relevant to the concerns of two particular groups: children with disabilities and professionals who need to co-ordinate their work with social services.

Children with Disabilities

Responses from parents, young people, social workers and carers who undertook assessments for the looked after group suggested from an early stage that the original Assessment and Action Records did not provide an adequate means of assessing the development and progress of children with physical and mental disabilities. This was not simply a criticism of the questions on health or education, but one which ran through the content of the other dimensions as well: identity, family and social relationships, emotional and behavioural development, social presentation and self care skills.

Users regularly identified three ways in which the original Assessment and Action Records failed to take account of the needs of children with disabilities. Firstly, the Records were based on an assumption that all children would have similar developmental goals and they were therefore damaging to the self-esteem of those who could not hope to match the progress of their able-bodied peers. Secondly, they failed to give due weight to issues such as communication and mobility which may be extremely significant for children with certain disabilities, but which the able-bodied take for granted. Thirdly, using the Records with children with disabilities brought us into a wider political debate concerning the relevance of the official guidance and regulations on assessment, plans and reviews for children who experience repeated periods of planned respite care (Department of Health, 1991c).

Initial enquiries as to how the Records might be adapted to meet the needs of children with disabilities produced the finding that potential users often objected strongly to undertaking this type of assessment in the first place. Although many users welcomed the introduction of detailed assessment tools for able-bodied children, the parents and carers of children with disabilities often found the whole concept difficult to accept.

The *Children Act 1989* sought to safeguard the well-being of children with disabilities by offering all those who lived away from home the same protection that had been previously extended only to those who were in the care of social services departments: in particular there is now a requirement to make plans and review arrangements for their care wherever they are living. However, many of these children spend the majority of their time with their families; the short periods of respite care offered through social services or health authorities are accepted as a means of lessening the strain on the family, but parents often regard the accompanying requirement to review the progress of children who make use of the service as an unwelcome and stigmatising intrusion. The detailed assessment of the arrangements for a child's day-to-day care and the monitoring of his or her progress required by the Assessment and Action Records can be seen by parents as offering an implied criticism of the quality of care they are providing (Department of Health, 1994a). Part of the problem lies in the implicit conflict to be found in providing an informal and flexible service that is also governed by stringent regulations. At the time of writing, these are being reviewed; nevertheless, even if they are relaxed, parents of children who have physical and emotional, but not necessarily social, needs may still regard them as stigmatising.

The research team had to try to distinguish between valid criticism of the materials we had produced and objections to the regulations under which they were being used. The introduction of the Records threw into sharp relief the difficulties in implementing these regulations. We passed on these findings to policy makers, but we decided not to become actively involved in the campaign to alter them; otherwise we would have lost our claim to impartiality and upset the balance of the dialogue between practitioners, policy makers and researchers, upon which the development of the materials relied.

Even after we had decided that our role should be restricted to dealing with the criticisms of the Records, trying to resolve some of the issues that had been raised proved to be a complex task. Obviously, we needed to alter the Assessment and Action Records in some way so that they could more nearly reflect the experiences of children with disabilities, but it was by no means clear how this might be done. Producing a different Record for them would be likely to create at least as many difficulties as it solved. There would be the problem of definition. There are no clear criteria for distinguishing between the disabled and the able-bodied: all children will fall somewhere on a continuum of ability and although it is relatively simple to identify those who sit at either end of the spectrum, it is virtually impossible to decide where a dividing line should be drawn. Many children experience some form of impairment, but this can range from a minor condition such as myopia to a major dysfunction such as paraplegia; moreover, the extent to which an impairment disables a child and the extent to which such a disability is perceived as a handicap will vary enormously and be dependent on a large number of extraneous factors. Deciding whose progress should be assessed on a Record designed for children with disabilities and whose should be assessed according to criteria designed for the able-bodied would be an arbitrary procedure which could have serious ethical implications.

Moreover, children with disabilities are children first and foremost: to assess their well-being and progress in a different manner from their able-bodied peers would inevitably concentrate a disproportionate amount of attention on their disability, although this may only affect one area of their development. It is, for instance, all too easy to assume that children and adults with physical disabilities which restrict their ability to communicate have impaired intellectual capacities, when this may be very far from the case. Such assumptions have produced low expectations for disabled children, which are inevitably detrimental to their progress.

The solution that, after extensive consultation, we initially decided to adopt was to produce a supplement which users could introduce in response to trigger questions from the mainstream Assessment and Action Records. For instance, if the mainstream question asking whether the child had regular physical exercise elicited the response that restricted mobility made it difficult for him or her to participate in sport, this would trigger further questions in the supplement, asking about access to physiotherapy and the provision of special aids and equipment. By ensuring that access to the questions designed specifically for children with disabilities could only be reached by using the mainstream Records, we sought to reinforce the view that these were 'children first and disabled second' and that their progress in those areas of development which were not affected by their disability should be assessed in the same way as that of able-bodied children. By placing questions that were only relevant to children with disabilities on a separate supplement, we sought to reduce the mainstream Records to a manageable size.

The supplement was briefly piloted in five local authorities. The response to its content was positive and it seemed as though we had produced assessment materials that addressed the needs of a wide range of children with varying abilities. However, our brief was not only to produce materials that addressed appropriate issues but to present them as practice tools that would be acceptable to users. We found that there were serious practical difficulties in using the supplement: some respondents completed it on its own and ignored the mainstream Record, others misunderstood the purpose of the triggers and almost all found it irritating and confusing to find their way through two documents at the same time, particularly if they were trying to produce a summary of future work alongside the two Records. On balance it seemed that the risk of alienating users by asking them to complete documents which contained some questions that would not be relevant to all the children they assessed was less than that of the supplementary section being misused or ignored and it was abandoned, the additional questions being incorporated into the mainstream Assessment and Action Records.

Collaboration with Other Professionals

When children are looked after away from home, several people take joint responsibility for their welfare; parents retain parental responsibility but this is also shared with the local authority and its various representatives. We had tried to reflect this situation by designing Assessment and Action Records that were intended to provide a structure by which all those responsible for children's care might assess their experiences and plan improvements in partnership with one another. Thus, the questions specifically include parents, social workers, foster carers, residential workers, health visitors and older children as people who might need to work together to meet deficits in the quality of care once they have been identified. It was the research on children with disabilities, who often need to make extensive use of services outside those provided by social workers, that initially alerted us to the need to co-ordinate the contents of the Records so that they dovetailed with structures in place in other agencies with responsibilities for children's welfare.

Although we were aware that individual children can often find that their needs have been overlooked when parental responsibilities are shared, we did not initially appreciate how those who are looked after can also miss out on the provisions that are collectively made for all children within a particular community. As is evident from the experiences of our community group, in spite of considerable retrenchment in recent years (cf YMCA, 1994), children living with their families still profit from a wide range of services provided both by public institutions and voluntary organisations, although there is considerable regional variation in their quality. We found, for instance, that children in one area we visited took part in a wide range of leisure activities offered by both the local authority and a local church; in another area, where there was less provision, they tended to make less varied use of their leisure time and to watch more television.

Looked after children often come from families that are poorly integrated into the local community and which tend to make little use of the services provided. One of the advantages to children of having the local authority as an official parent should be that they receive optimal opportunities to make use of its services, not only within the social services department, but also within education, housing and leisure. Moreover, the local authority should be in a stronger position than other parents to ensure that its children benefit from the services provided by other agencies, such as the health authority.

The feedback from the evaluation study suggested, however, that this was often not the case. One major obstacle which prevents looked after children from making full use of services is the frequency with which they move. Anyone who has ever moved house with children will know the potentially damaging effects of the upheaval. Settling into a new school is only part of the problem: making new friends, finding a dentist and getting into the Saturday football squad require just as much time and effort, not only from the children themselves, but also from their carers. The children and young people aged over seven in our looked after group had experienced a median number of three placements *during the period that they had been looked after*; the children and young people of this age in our community group had experienced a median of one change of address *in their lives*. This being so, it is not surprising that the looked after children were less well integrated into the communities in which they lived than their peers.

Looked after children do not only find it difficult to make use of services because they frequently change address. There is also evidence to suggest that, far from opening doors to greater provision, the process of being looked after can close them. Major difficulties can be caused by the antagonisms that often exist between departments: it is not uncommon, for instance, to find authorities which have difficulties in assessing and reviewing looked after children because education departments refuse to collaborate with social services. The frequency of such antagonisms and the damage they do has been documented by Lyon (1991). The needs of looked after children can also be overlooked if information structures are inadequate; for instance, there is evidence that they are more likely to be excluded from school than those living with their families (Dennis and Erdos, 1993) yet social services departments are not required to keep statistics on school exclusions amongst their looked after population and so this information is often not available to those who negotiate with education departments. And yet it would strengthen their arguments immensely: for example, one in five of the children aged over ten in our looked after group had been excluded in the six months prior to assessment.

Research from health authorities reinforces the view that looked after children lose out on provision because of insufficient dialogue between the organisations responsible for their care. An audit undertaken in one health authority in 1992 found that, although the *Children Act 1989* now requires all looked after children to have a written health plan and to be given regular medical examinations, they had only received details of 49% of children looked after by the local authority. Moreover, in those cases where information was available, it was often very sketchy; in over 50% of all cases, health personnel had no information about the child's birth family or whether there was a family history of inheritable disorder; in over 75% of all cases there was no information about the child's legal status, care history or length of time they had been looked after; no information was gathered either before or during the health examinations about the dental care of any of the children, nor were any growth charts plotted (Payne *et al*, 1992).

All agencies which provide services for children share the aim of promoting their welfare. Yet where the dialogue between agencies is inadequate, confusion inevitably arises concerning the roles that representatives from different professions are expected to fulfil. This confusion is likely to reinforce existing antagonisms. The original Assessment and Action Records asked for details of the child's height, weight and growth rates. The accompanying guidelines gave examples of centile charts and pointed out that the growth rates of vulnerable children should be plotted by health visitors, general practitioners or school nurses. The guidance concluded by telling social workers that they 'should make certain that growth charts of vulnerable children *are* being kept and updated; if not, it is advisable to keep a chart on the file and plot height and weight yourself' (Department of Health, 1991a). This suggestion proved extremely controversial and was removed in the second edition of the guidelines on the grounds that centile charts are difficult to interpret and to encourage their completion by social workers, who might not understand them, would raise more difficulties than it solved. When we came to look at the data from the looked after group, we also found that, although height and weight were regularly measured, in only very few cases was an attempt made to calculate the centile on which children fell; the revised Records no longer ask for this information.

Yet the issue cannot be resolved simply by taking this responsibility away from social workers, for the evidence from the health authority audit shows that in none of the statutory medical examinations for looked after children did health professionals plot centiles either. The findings from our looked after group suggest that while the growth rates of a few, seriously underweight children were being carefully monitored, little attention was being given to the considerable numbers of adolescents in residential care who were over-weight. If, as we believe, growth rates can provide clear indicators of well-being for vulnerable children, adequate arrangements need to be made for monitoring them.

Although close collaboration between all agencies responsible for children's welfare is now recognised as leading to better outcomes, once a child is in care or accommodation it is frequently social services which undertake most of the work. The extensive consultation with health and education professionals illustrates some of the difficulties. Our purpose was to produce revised materials that could be used to promote partnerships between the various agencies responsible for children's welfare as well as between the individuals with whom care is shared. Agencies have different priorities and expectations of the way in which the finished product should be used; a major part of our task was to reconcile a number of conflicting agendas. For instance, health professionals advised us that extensive guidance should be included on issues such as diet, exercise and alcohol; yet when we came to draft this on to the Assessment and Action Records, it became apparent that in doing so we were converting an assessment tool into a health promotion exercise. Although the Records are rightly seen as an effective method of conveying research messages to practitioners by indicating which issues need to be covered, their purpose is to assess children's experiences and progress; consequently, we dropped much of the guidance on health promotion on the grounds that it deflected attention away from the assessment procedure.

The greatest difficulty lay in producing materials that covered the key issues which a variety of agencies regarded as fundamental to children's development, without extending them until they were too lengthy for practitioners to use. Inevitably, we have had to omit some issues in order to include others. We have, however, been at pains to revise the materials in such a way that they reinforce the point that social services departments need to work in co-ordination with other agencies to meet their responsibilities for looked after children. The guidance notes included in the revised materials reiterate the recommendation that statutory medicals should be organised through a designated medical adviser who also has responsibility for monitoring their outcome and for checking that recommendations are carried out; the guidance also underlines the official recommendations that close alliances between education and social services should be fostered at all levels (Home Office *et al*, 1991; Department for Education, 1994). It supports the proposal that a designated educational adviser should be nominated in each department to deal with these issues. At the grass roots level, we have included health visitors, school nurses and educators among the group of front-line carers who might be expected to share responsibility for particular 'parental' actions.

It is to everyone's advantage that an assessment and monitoring system used by social services should complement, rather than reiterate or overlap, systems in use by other, related, services. We have therefore been at pains to relate the Assessment and Action Records and accompanying materials to the Personal Child Health Records which are in use in about 60% of health authorities. We have also attempted to align the *Looking After Children* materials with the requirements of the National Curriculum, Standard Attainment Targets in schools and the *Education Act 1993*. Although these are only small initiatives, the aim is that the materials should promote partnerships between different agencies as well as between the various people who share responsibility for the children concerned.

Towards a Blueprint of Parental Tasks and Responsibilities

It was the decision to develop the Assessment and Action Records as a practice tool that prevented us from reducing their length. Had they been developed solely for research purposes it would have been relatively easy to pick out the key variables that local authorities need to monitor in order to be reassured that the children for whom they are responsible are progressing satisfactorily and that resources are being accurately targeted: such an exercise would have reduced the Records to the assessments of objectives that now occur at the end of each of the seven dimensions, embellished perhaps by a few additional questions about problematic behaviour and its management.

These are the parts of the Records that will provide useful aggregate data when they come to be computerised.

However, while a research record can and probably should, be pruned until only the significant variables remain, the same is not true of a practice tool. Children and young people, carers and social workers do not use the materials to gather data, but as a framework for assessing the quality of parenting provided. As a blueprint to guide those responsible through the complexities of the parental task, the Records need to reflect its multi-faceted nature. The results from the evaluation study have shown that while a number of individual questions can cause controversy, there is a broad consensus that the Records cover the relevant issues. In two years of extensive enquiry, we were only advised that two or three questions in the original materials were not essential and should be removed. This point was reinforced by the feedback from parents and children in the community study.

It is possible to argue that certain aspects of parenting are more important than others. After all, some issues such as the provision of food, are matters of life and death while others, such as the ability to go on school outings, are not. However if, as the original working party argued, bringing up children is not only about keeping them alive but also about providing the opportunities they need to enable them to achieve satisfactory well-being in adulthood and if local authorities should be emulating the tasks of ordinary parents rather than providing a service based on considerations of less eligibility, then they are accountable for fulfilling more extensive responsibilities.

Some of the criticisms about the content of the Records indicate a need to open up a debate about the standards of parenting which it might be appropriate for public authorities to follow. In recent years there has been considerable concern expressed both by politicians and academics that parents are increasingly uncertain of their responsibilities. Although this issue has been vociferously taken up by the political right as a reason for reducing welfare benefits, concerns about cultural relativism and the erosion of responsibility have also been expressed in less emotive terms by serious academics (e.g. Dennis and Erdos, 1993; Halsey, 1993; Hewitt, 1993). There does seem to be a genuine case for arguing that our understanding of the precise nature of parental responsibilities has become confused.

Feedback from social workers in the evaluation study suggested that there is an even greater vacuum in our understanding of the parental responsibilities which public bodies should undertake and that this vacuum is open to appropriation by a number of different lobbies, each with their axe to grind. Local authorities need to offer their staff some guidance as to where, as corporate parents, they stand on controversial issues concerning, for instance, homosexuality or children's rights. In common with all parents, local authorities also need to have some strategy on how to resolve the inevitable conflict between children's immediate wishes and their long-term interests. They also need to discuss these questions with those people with whom they share parental responsibility; we found all too frequently that social workers who held strong ideological views themselves made erroneous assumptions about parental aspirations for the children for whom they were responsible. Responses from some social workers to the questions that ask about educational support would come under this category. The revised Assessment and Action Records attempt to provide a basis for the work that local authorities should be undertaking in their role as parents; inevitably they contain the biases of the researchers who produced them, but the questions are based on the results of a wide body of serious academic research and have now been tested on a group of children and parents in the community. They undoubtedly provide a more objective blueprint than has previously been available.

Conclusion

As far as we are aware, the Assessment and Action Records represent the first attempt to provide a comprehensive methodology for assessing the experiences and progress of children looked after away from home. The original Records were experimental documents and it is not surprising that the evaluation study revealed a need for the large number of adjustments described above. The revised edition is based on objective information from extensive field trials as well as considerably more consultation than the original; we therefore expect it to have relevance for a longer period. There is, however, a number of reasons why it, or indeed any edition, is unlikely to become the definitive and permanent version.

Firstly, we have developed the instruments as practice tools. We do not yet know how accurate is the information they obtain, nor will we do so until they have been more extensively used. This is an issue that will be given further consideration in Chapter Eight.

Secondly, while research has identified many of the parental inputs which lead to successful outcomes in health and education, the extent of our knowledge of issues such as how parents can help children acquire self-confidence or learn to make friends is still relatively limited. Questions in some of the dimensions are based more on experience than on objective research; as our knowledge about effective parenting increases, alterations will need to be made. We have already replaced some of the original questions on the emotional and behavioural development and the family and social relationships dimensions with questions which have been validated in other research projects; we expect that this could be a continuing procedure as further research findings become available. Similarly, as our knowledge of the experiences of looked after children improves, issues which had previously been overlooked will need to be addressed; 15 years ago, for example, the Records would have contained no reference to sexual abuse.

Finally, although we are reasonably confident that progress along the seven dimensions leads to long-term well-being in adulthood, we have defined well-being in the context of British society in the 1990s. Different social conditions are likely to require a change of emphasis. For instance, in societies where welfare provisions are minimal and survival is the overriding preoccupation, helping children to acquire a strong sense of identity may well be regarded as a frivolous side issue compared with the need to ensure that they are sufficiently healthy and acquire appropriate skills to take their place in the labour market. In cultures where there is internal conflict, a strong sense of identity with a particular faction may indeed be regarded as undesirable. Evidence from the community group, discussed in the following chapter, does, however, further our understanding of those issues which parents and children in Britain regard as important today.

Summary Points

1. The contents of the Records were revised on the basis of evidence of their limitations as a practice tool. Responses on Assessment and Action Records completed for the looked after study and the community group, feedback from specialist advisers and both formal and informal comments from users were all influential in directing the process of revision.

2. Academic alterations to the Records included the introduction of improved indicators of emotional disturbance. Other alterations were informed by current ideological debates. The third type of alteration concerned the need to broaden the relevance of the Records to the concerns of particular users.

3. A major alteration was the adaptation of the Records to address more closely the needs of children with disabilities. The original version was seen to reinforce a sense of failure for children who could not hope to match the developmental progress of their peers and to overlook issues such as communication and mobility which the able-bodied take for granted. The original Records have been extended to include supplementary questions which address these issues, other options having been rejected on ethical or practical grounds.

4. Although the local authority, in its capacity as a corporate parent, should be in a strong position to ensure that the children for whom it is responsible benefit from the services provided by other agencies, the community group tended to make better use of them than the looked after children. Poor relationships between social services departments and other agencies can create barriers for looked after children: the Records have been amended to try to improve collaboration by linking with health and education assessments.

5. There is a need for more open debate about the standards of parenting which it might be appropriate for local authorities to provide. A lack of clear direction leaves a vacuum that is easily appropriated by groups with a particular axe to grind. Objections that the questions on education reflected middle class values that have little relevance for looked after children appear to derive from an ideology that needs to be challenged. The Records provide a comprehensive blueprint which serves as a focus for such a debate.

Chapter 4

Identifying standards of parenting

Introduction

The *Children Act 1989* states that:

> It shall be the duty of a local authority looking after any child
> (a) to safeguard and promote his welfare; and
> (b) to make such use of services available for children cared for by their own parents as appears to the authority to be reasonable in his case (S.22.3).

By giving local authorities a duty to provide a standard of care similar to that which one would expect of a reasonable parent, the Act creates an opportunity to break with the persistent tradition of less eligibility inherited from the Poor Law. The Assessment and Action Records were based on the premise inherent in the Act: that rather than confining their efforts to the prevention of further harm, statutory agencies should provide enhanced opportunities for the children for whom they share responsibilities. The Records therefore set out those opportunities which research indicates that reasonable parents should offer in order to help their children attain long-term well-being in adulthood. In doing this, the working party found it necessary to make a number of assumptions about those things which are important to ordinary parents and the way in which they set about their task; an immediate criticism was that the Records simply reflected the liberal, middle class views of the working party members.

It was evident that such criticisms could only be addressed by finding out more about the aims of ordinary parents and how they set about achieving them. Four of the Records (for ages 3–4; 5–9; 10–15 and 16 and over) were therefore tested by using them in interviews with children and families living in the community. In the previous chapter we demonstrated how this information was used to refine and develop the materials. However, in examinimg the relevance of the Records to the concerns of ordinary families, we also gathered a wealth of data about the way in which children are brought up in Britain today. Much of this information has relevance outside this study and we do not have the space to do it justice here. It will therefore be analysed and further discussed in later publications. In this chapter we show how information about the practices of ordinary families can be used to provide some benchmarks in the discussion about appropriate standards for local authorities. As will become evident, we discovered very few differences between social classes about what parents consider important.

Caution has been exercised in reporting any empirical findings. The children were selected in order to test four age-banded Records and their ages are not, therefore, respresentative of all children in the community. Nevertheless, their circumstances do provide information about the situations and experiences of ordinary families. It is also important to note that the looked after group was not constructed in such a way as to draw a direct comparison with the community group because most social services departments selected subgroups whom they considered it particularly useful to assess; however, as this chapter demonstrates, the data collected so far indicate those areas which merit further exploration with a randomly selected sample of children in care or accommodation.

Profile of the Community Group

Data on the community group came from completing Assessment and Action Records with 379 children and their carers. The children were clustered around ages 3–4, 8–9, 12–13 and

16–17. Sampling was undertaken by contacting representative secondary and infant schools in two of the local authorities assessing children in the looked after group.

The families came from a wide range of occupational groups, as the following table, based on the Registrar General's classification, shows:

Table 4.1: *Occupational Classification of Employed Parents in the Community Group*

Classification	Number of fathers	Percentage of fathers	Number of mothers	Percentage of mothers
Higher professional	18	7%	1	0.4%
Lower professional	75	29%	53	23%
Routine non-manual skilled manual	84	33%	71	31%
Semi-skilled manual	36	14%	17	7%
Unskilled manual	42	16%	90	39%

Fifteen per cent of the fathers were unemployed; a considerable proportion of them had been out of work for several years. Most employed mothers were in part-time jobs, though a third worked full-time. Over half the young people over the age of 13 were also in part-time employment, which included regular paper rounds, Saturday jobs or evening shop work. Employment is important for young and old alike; it not only gives teenagers extra income, it also increases their skills, self-esteem and confidence and provides opportunities for contacts and support outside the home. Information about work and work experience was not routinely collected about young people looked after, although the Assessment and Action Records have now been amended to do this. About 10% of households had incomes of less than £5,000 per year, and a similar proportion had incomes over £26,000; within this range, they followed a normal distribution.

The ethnic profile of the community group was similar to that of the general population; 94% were white and 6% came from minority ethnic groups: this includes 4% who were of mixed parentage. However, these children came from very diverse backgrounds.

Seventy-two per cent of the children lived with both parents, while 20% were in households headed by a lone parent and 8% were living with a step-parent. However, all but two children and young people lived with at least one birth parent; the exceptions were one 17-year-old who lived with grandparents and one 16-year-old who was living independently. Ninety-six per cent lived with brothers and sisters and a further 15% shared their homes with grandparents, cousins, aunts and uncles and in one case the young person's wife. Hence, household size ranged from one (the 16-year-old girl who lived alone) to eleven; over half the children lived in families with four or five members.

Bebbington and Miles (1989) identified six distinguishing characteristics of children who come into care or accommodation. These were: household head receives income support; child lives in a single adult household; four or more children in the household; child of mixed ethnic origin; family living in a privately rented home; one or more persons per room. The odds of a child from a family displaying all six indicators being looked after by a local authority are one in ten, while those displaying none of these indicators have just a one in 7,000 chance of being looked after. Just over half (53%) the community group had none of the characteristics identified by Bebbington and Miles, while one in four (27%) had two or more. Since the main criticism of the Records was that they set standards that did not reflect the experiences of looked after children, we were particularly interested to discover whether families that displayed these characteristics differed in their practices from others in the community.

Two features, separation and subsequent mobility, distinguish children in care or accommodation from those in the community and were of particular relevance to this study.

Looked after children already have to cope with living apart from their families; changes of placement, disruptions and periods placed with parents mean that many experience instability throughout their childhood; this is particularly characteristic of those who stay long in care. For example, our looked after group had experienced an average of three moves since admission to care or accommodation, a finding which is echoed by other studies (Fitzgerald, 1987; Rowe et al, 1989). Since separation and mobility are seen as major impediments to the progress of children in care or accommodation, we were interested to see how families coped with similar difficulties. Almost all the children in the community group had lived with at least one parent all their lives; 37% had also lived at the same address, thereby emphasising the contrast with a looked after group. However, a small group of 16 children (4%) had experienced separation in hospital or had lived with other relatives for a month or more; another group of 49 (13%) children had lived at three or more addresses.We were particularly interested to see how these experiences had influenced the way in which children were brought up. The following analysis looks more closely at the community group as a whole, and attempts to draw some conclusions about particular subgroups within it.

Health

There are many indicators of good health, but height and weight are good starting points. As expected, a small proportion (4%) of the children were under the third centile for height; however less than half of those who were not growing satisfactorily had been referred for treatment. Children's weight was a greater problem than height. One in ten were either clinically underweight (less than the 3rd centile), or grossly overweight (i.e. more than the 97th centile). Sixty-one per cent ate sweets or crisps every day and 16% ate no fresh fruit. Parents' perceptions about diet were consonant with these findings: over a fifth thought children were receiving a less than adequate diet. Children who suffered economic deprivation were more likely to have an unhealthy diet than their peers: 78% of those whose parents were on income support ate sweets every day and 27% ate no fresh fruit. However, diet was also closely related to age: as children grew older parents began to feel that they had little control over their eating and complained that there was too much encouragement to eat chips and junk food at school.

A quarter (25%) of the children in the community group had not visited a dentist in the six months prior to assessment, although three-fifths (63%) were waiting for an appointment. As Chapter Three has indicated, a number of parents and carers regarded children's short-term wishes as a valid reason for allowing them to take actions that might be detrimental to their future well-being: this accounted for 19% of non-attendance in the community group. These findings held across the age range and were not confined to older adolescents.

The Health of the Nation (Department of Health, 1992) aims to achieve a 95% uptake of childhood immunisation by 1995. This improves on the 90% uptake reached in May 1992. All the 3-4 year olds were up-to-date with their immunisations. However, local Regional Health Authorities' policy to offer BCG immunisation only to those at risk of contracting tuberculosis meant that half the children had not received protection from TB. Girls were also asked whether they were safeguarded against rubella; though this vaccination has been available for a number of years, it emerged that 5% of the appropriate age group were unprotected.

While much child care research has focused on questions of abuse, the greatest risk to the safety of children is from accidents. The Health of the Nation states that: 'Accidents are the leading cause of death amongst children and young people. The consequences of some accidents can be life-long disability or a predisposition to ill-health later in life. Action to reduce accidents will have a significant effect on the health and well-being of children.' (Department of Health, 1992). It is young children who are particularly vulnerable to accidental injury. Seventy per cent of burns and scalding accidents occur in children under five and these result in about 5,000 hospital admissions and 100 deaths each year (BSI and Child Accident Prevention Trust, 1994). Yet three fifths (58%) of the parents of 3–4 year-olds did not use a fireguard where necessary and 12% of these younger children were at risk in the kitchen from unguarded saucepans and trailing electrical flexes.

Every year approximately 14,000 children, the majority of whom are under five, are admitted to hospital after ingesting poisonous substances; yet medicines and cleaning fluids were accessible to nearly one in ten 3-4 year-olds; it is perhaps unsurprising that 16% had been treated at a hospital for accidental injuries in the 12 months prior to assessment. Further analysis showed that the higher the levels of deprivation in the home (using the Bebbington and Miles criteria) the less likely parents were to protect their children by using a fireguard, keeping poisons out of reach or providing adequate kitchen safety.

Most of the young people did, however, take sensible precautions to keep themselves safe; 85% of ten to 16 year olds living with both parents were conscious of the fact that they should get a taxi home or arrange to be collected if they were going out for the evening. They were aware of the dangers of walking home alone or putting themselves in other vulnerable situations, although most girls were found to be more prepared than boys. However, young people in step-families or living with a lone parent made fewer conscious efforts to protect themselves.

It was found that one in ten of the community group had experienced some kind of abuse, often bullying at school; for some, these experiences resulted in their taking extra self-protective measures:

> Jane was 12 when we interviewed her and was living with both her parents. She had a mild learning difficulty and had been badly bullied at school. Recently, however, she had been going to judo classes and was developing much more confidence in her ability to take care of herself physically. This confidence was

also affecting other parts of her life too, and was enabling her to engage more positively with her peer group.

In summary, the children in the community group were generally healthy. Although there were virtually no differences across social classes, the evidence from the study reveals some concerns about diet, dental hygiene, immunisations and protection from accidents or abuse. A number of these issues could be taken up by health authorities in their efforts to bring up to standard the situation of ordinary children in the community. The data also suggest that, if the children for whom they share responsibility are to improve their chances of achieving long-term well-being, local authorities need to set a higher standard of health care than that which prevails in some families. The experiences of the looked after group, who appeared to have a better diet and safer homes than some of their peers, would suggest that this is already accepted: this is one of the issues which should be explored further.

Education

The Records for 3–4 year olds asked how often children had access to stimulating toys, drawing or writing materials and books, as well as how much time adults spent with them, talking, reading or playing. All children between three and five in the community group had access to playthings and drawing materials more than once a week and nearly all spent over half their waking day talking to or playing with adults. All were learning to count, recognise objects and follow simple instructions; all were read to several times a week, 90% of them daily. However, 4% of 3–4 year olds owned less than ten books, 11% were not learning to recognise words and 10% were not developing speech adequately.

These findings suggest that parents are generally aware of the importance of providing a stimulating environment for young children and of preparing them for school. The proportion who were not receiving intellectual stimulation was extremely small: there were no differences in social class or indicators of deprivation except that children who were read to less frequently and were not being taught to recognise words were slightly more likely to come from large families where, presumably, adults had less time to provide additional stimulation.

In general, parents continued to provide educational support after children had started school. Most children and young people got help with schoolwork at home and had somewhere reasonably quiet to do their homework. However, there was again evidence that not every child was receiving a high standard of care. Of particular concern were the eight children (5%) of secondary school age who had been excluded from school in the six months that preceded the interviews. The education offered in these circumstances was frequently unsatisfactory, often being reduced to one or two hours home tuition every week. Other children had no-one to attend parents' evenings on their behalf, and about one in ten had limited access to books. The mother of one nine-year-old told the interviewer: 'There's no point in going up to the school or talking to them — it's a waste of time. He brings books home which I can't read so what good is that?'

There was a discernible link between movement and educational outcome: 43% of the children who had changed address three times or more had also changed schools. Children who had lived at more than three addresses also featured disproportionately in the group who had been excluded from school; although one would need to know more about the reasons for frequent moves, the evidence adds weight to the view that they have a detrimental effect in themselves and may be a contributory factor to the poor educational attainments so often noted for children in care or accommodation On the other hand, deprivation appeared to be a greater contributory factor to poor educational attainment than did instability: children with four or more recognised indicators of deprivation were over-represented amongst the exclusions and were also less likely to be learning to swim or to play a musical instrument.

The evidence on children in the community demonstrates a number of ways in which parents seek to ensure reasonable educational outcomes for their children, which professionals might find helpful. Most parents tried to avoid disrupting children's education when they moved house, and they managed to sustain children's extra-curricular activities in spite of a change of address. A higher proportion of children in the community group appeared to be performing at above average levels than might have been predicted from their socio-demographic characteristics. Although this may be due to sampling bias, it could also be the case that parents over-estimated their children's abilities, especially as we were not able to verify their assessments of academic attainment with schools. Parents also paid attention to the non-academic tasks of education such as learning to swim, to ride a bicycle and to play a musical instrument, all of which help improve children's self-confidence. Even though it is not based on a random sample, the evidence from the looked after group suggests that educational inputs for looked after children lag behind their peers in a number of areas, a point that has frequently been made by other researchers (eg Colton, Jackson and Heath, 1994; Jackson, 1994).

Identity

As children gradually separate themselves from parents or primary carers and create their own sense of self, their identity develops. For all children, these transitions are difficult: roles within the family frequently change; children's roles in society also change, and their perception of themselves will be altered, not only by belonging to a different group but also by the expectations and judgements of its members. The importance of identity for long-term well-being explains its place in the Assessment and Action Records.

Knowledge about personal circumstances is fundamental to the development of an informed sense of self. Almost all the children in the community group knew their names, addresses and birthdays; however, nearly 10% of those who were not living with both parents were uncertain of their situation. Families where there was a resident step-parent had particular difficulties in being open about the ways in which adults and children were related.

About a quarter of the children (28%) in the community group lacked self-confidence; children who did not know why they were not living with both parents were over-represented on this variable, which was more closely related to family structure than to economic deprivation. The interviews revealed that, whilst some young people seemed to have an intrinsic belief in their own self worth and effectiveness, many lost confidence in specific situations, for instance at school. Others were perfectly confident at home and school but found social situations demanding. Giving children responsibility for simple tasks such as setting the table for dinner or feeding a pet and praising them for doing it well was found to be helpful in developing children's self-confidence, as was reading and talking to young children and encouraging them to join clubs to develop their particular interests. If professionals bear these findings in mind while completing the Records, the situation of many looked after children could be improved.

The Records asked children and young people over the age of five to say what things they think they are good at. Those who had little self-confidence found it difficult to answer these questions, which provided a valuable means of getting children to talk about themselves and their interests. Parents were able to use these questions to encourage children to think more positively about themselves: for instance, when a child of seven could not think of anything he was good at, his mother talked to him about how patient and kind he was with younger children and said how much they liked him.

A young person who is confident at home will have better success at securing a stable life outside it. When asked what their plans and hopes were for the future, most young people in the community group were concerned about jobs and qualifications. Only 18% of the 16–17 year-olds had begun to think about moving away from their families.

Many of the issues dealt with in this section of the Records cause more difficulties to children and young people in care or accommodation, whose sense of identity may be damaged by the experiences that have led to their being looked after away from home. The responses from the community group confirm that these issues are also of importance to children who live with their families; however parents have learnt particular strategies for helping them to develop self-esteem and confidence.

One area where the strategies developed within a community might be usefully compared with those developed by social services centres around the reluctance of step-families to discuss separation from a birth parent; another is the way in which adolescents prepare themselves psychologically for the future: the evidence suggests that while those in the community are planning future occupations and qualifications, those looked after may be devoting their energies to worrying about their relationships with family members or their ability to cope with early independence.

Family and Social Relationships

Relationships with family members provide children with 'a framework for interpreting experience and teach them how to negotiate meaning in a manner congruent with the requirements of the culture' (Bruner and Haste, 1987). Although nearly all those in the community group were closely attached to their mother and/or father the Records revealed a number of difficulties in their relationships. Our expectation that displays of physical affection would be fewer as children grew older was confirmed by the responses from teenagers, but we also found that one in eight children under ten were not regularly hugged or cuddled by their parents. Explanations for such a parenting style included 'he doesn't deserve it' or 'she does not like it'. Some families were simply undemonstrative. A high proportion of 3–4 year- olds (38%) needed a comfort object; children who were identified as having been maltreated were over-represented in this group. Children receiving less physical affection were more likely to be living in two-parent households suggesting that lone and step-parents compensate children for disadvantage, or possibly come to rely on their children for emotional support and succour.

Support from members of the extended family was a major resource for children in the community and likely to be one that differentiated them from those in care or accommodation: over 50% of them saw not only grandparents but also aunts, uncles and other family members at least once a week. Where families were dispersed, children were encouraged to maintain contact by letter or telephone. It was also common for children living in their own families to have a wide network of people other than family members, to whom they could turn for help and advice. A friend's mother, their mother's friend or a neighbour they had known all their lives frequently took on this role.

It is possible to trace a relationship between children's social perceptions of themselves and their sense of self-esteem: those who lacked confidence in other areas also felt they had few friends; they were also slightly more likely to come from step- or single-parent families. The data from this section further highlight the value of questions in the Records about the quality and depth of relationships with family and friends. Perceptions about relationships should, however, be regarded with some caution: in particular it is important to distinguish between instant, superficial friendships that are easily discarded and are characteristic of young people who have had few opportunities to form secure and consistent attachments and the ability to develop and sustain more intimate relationships.

Social Presentation, Emotional and Behavioural Development

In the past, children in care could be distinguished from their counterparts by their appearance and behaviour in public; in the nineteenth and early twentieth centuries they often wore uniform, were almost always much cleaner than their peers and were expected to be more regimented and more polite than those in the community. Today, our expectations are that all children will receive 'that care which it would be reasonable to expect a parent to provide'; the Records are designed to discover whether children in care or accommodation are given opportunities to be part of the crowd and to dress and behave in the same way as their contemporaries. Evidence from the community group tells us more about parents' expectations for their children's behaviour and appearance.

Over 90% of children and young people in the community group were judged by the interviewers to look 'well cared for'. Although there were a small number of children, particularly in the older age groups, who disagreed with parents about how they should dress or wear their hair, there was a surprising lack of conflict about these issues. Many young people were also uncertain about how they should look and behave on important occasions, 11% saying that they would like more advice about what to wear and say at job or college interviews. Neither did we find much evidence of consistently inappropriate behaviour in public, although 8% of the children found it difficult to adjust their demeanour to different social situations. It should, however, be noted that parents' perceptions of the impression made by their children were not always accurate: the mother of one four-year-old regarded her son's behaviour as acceptable to adults, though the researcher recorded that: 'throughout the interview, the child hit and kicked me and his mother. He also threw things at me and his mother, would come up to me and smother my face, take things from my bag and not give them back and would then throw them round the room.'

Examples such as the above remind us that emotional and behavioural difficulties are by no means exclusive to children in care or accommodation. Rutter (1975) has written that: 'numerous studies have attested to the fact that most children show isolated psychological problems at one time or another and that many have transient periods of emotional disturbance or behavioural difficulties. To a considerable extent these are part and parcel of growing up and are not in themselves a cause for concern'. About a quarter of younger children in the community group showed clinging behaviour or had fears or nervous habits such as biting nails or twitches; a small proportion (2%) expressed distress by soiling or were unable to play normally (3%).

The Records cover behaviours that are outwardly destructive, such as the various types of aggression, as well as those that are potentially damaging to the individual, such as drug or alcohol abuse. Serious conduct problems were rare, and we came across only one young man who had been involved in assault or threatening behaviour, although 14% of the young people were sometimes aggressive and a further 6% were extremely irritable. We know that young people who feel unable to influence external events in their lives are more likely to direct their aggression at themselves. In some of the cases we looked at we saw these traits coalesce, as the following older teenager illustrates:

> Rick had a number of problems which included drug and alcohol abuse. He had been in trouble with the police after he had stolen a car and gone 'joy-riding' in it, following which he had been arrested and charged. He had left school without taking his exams and was working at a casual job in a garage. Relationships with his father and step-father were very tense though he did have a close (if at times strained) relationship with his mother whom he 'loved to bits' and a steady girlfriend with whom he was intending to marry and start a family.

> In the past Rick had taken two overdoses. At the time of the interview he was getting no help from anyone. 'Mum nags me about alcohol and my stepfather gets angry.'

Ben, in contrast was more fortunate. He was 12 when we interviewed him with his parents. The family had been having financial difficulties and were receiving income support because Ben's father was having problems maintaining his business. There had been considerable strain on the family during this time, since both parents were very worried about what was going to happen to them.

> Ben had always been disruptive in the family and presently there were frequent battles over food. He was 'always being sent out of his class and disturbing other children'. He would seek attention by 'stripping off to his pants and walking around the class'. He also 'makes the most noise in a crowd; goes the fastest and

furthest and will have a go at anything'. Furthermore, he was truanting from school regularly and had recently been in trouble with the police for shoplifting. When he was at school he would avoid doing the work and homework. His parents said that things worsened when he went to senior school but there had been trouble before. He had been suspended from junior school for three days for swearing at a dinner lady.

Ben's problems, however, were mixed and he also showed signs of emotional disturbance. For instance he had difficulty sleeping and was often extremely quiet and withdrawn. He had nervous twitches and his parents complained that he could not keep still or concentrate. There were also tensions and difficulties in the relationships Ben had with both parents and siblings. Though it was apparent that Ben's parents wanted to love him, they found it more and more difficult to have warm and affectionate contact with him and said that he had increasingly negative feelings about himself.

A protective factor in Ben's life was his relationship with his form tutor at the senior school, who was very supportive and had organised a referral to a psychologist. Since then Ben's situation had gradually improved. Ben's parents were, however, among several in the community group who described how difficult they had found it to get help for their children. Their greatest problem was not so much that they were unable to pay for services but that they had no knowledge of what was available, what would be appropriate or indeed what a psychologist or psychiatrist actually does or how they might be contacted.

These data are a reminder that emotional and behavioural problems are not the preserve of children supported by social services departments. There was no clear association with movement, separation, family structure or multiple deprivation, although there was a correlation between behaviour problems and poverty. The provision of specialist services should be one area in which local authorities with their knowledge, power and contacts, ought to be able to provide a better service than parents, only about half of whom succeeded in arranging their child's referral; evidence from the looked after group suggests that this is an issue that should be explored further as there are worrying suggestions that social workers find it difficult to accept that children and young people may need more than 'tender loving care' or 'talking to' if they are to overcome what are often serious emotional difficulties, and so refrain from referring children to specialist services.

Self Care Skills

The Records ask whether the children assessed have acquired a number of self care skills appropriate to their age and stage of development. We had expected differences in family structure to affect the acquisition of self care skills on the grounds that children from lone parent families might be given a greater share of practical responsibilities and those from reconstituted families might be more likely to be planning to leave home earlier. Although we did find that children from step-families had more concrete plans to leave after they reached 16, there was no evidence that they were better prepared to do so, as was demonstrated by the finding that 17% did not do the washing up. Overall, 91% of the community group had developed self care skills appropriate to their age, but there were no features that distinguished them from the 9% who had not.

Using the Records with Children in Need

Evidence from the community group demonstrates that it is possible to use the Assessment and Action Records with children living at home, as well as with those in care or accommodation, and to good effect. The interviewers found that, except in one or two cases where they doubted parents' veracity, the Records were an effective means of identifying difficulties and discussing how to address them. It was also relatively easy to use them to identify children and young people whose multiple difficulties placed them at considerable risk, as the following case history demonstrates:

> Winston was seventeen when we interviewed him. He was living at home with his parents, both of whom were in work. However, he had loose attachments to his family and was having difficulty

in making stable relationships or trusting anyone. He was of mixed race and was uncertain which ethnic group he belonged to; as a child he had tried to hang himself after being bullied because he was black.

Winston was asthmatic and overweight. He had few friends, none from his ethnic background. He had left school at 16 with six GCSEs, none of them grade C or above, and had had three jobs since then. He was now in college doing a welding course. He had recently been admitted to hospital because of a drinking problem which, he claimed, was due to abuse. Other behavioural problems included difficulty in trusting anyone, inappropriate sexual behaviour and drug abuse. He had been in trouble with the police and charged with an offence within the last six months. He was not receiving counselling or advice to cope with any of his manifest difficulties.

Conclusion

The above analysis has, of necessity, dwelt on those families that did not provide their children with the standard of care recommended by the Records. However, questions about the ways in which parenting differs between families and across social groups should not obscure the fact that almost all children were offered those opportunities considered necessary to ensure their long-term well-being within each of the seven dimensions. In focusing on the families which failed to meet the criteria, we are looking at a very small minority.

Moreover, the evidence from the community group suggests that many of the assumptions about parental practices made in the Assessment and Action Records are already widely recognised as a key to effective parenting. Parents from all walks of life are, for instance, now aware that if they want their children to do well at school, they need to read to them and give them access to books. They are also generally aware of the relationship between diet and health and of the damaging effects of smoking. The differences lie in the extent to which they feel able to make use of this knowledge. Some parents do not have the money to provide resources such as a nutritious diet (see also National Children's Home, 1991). Others lack the confidence or the academic skills needed to foster their children's education. They may also be hampered by resentment about their own unhappy school experiences. Other parents do not feel that they have the authority to encourage their children to follow a particular path, particularly if, over issues such as smoking and drinking, they have been unable themselves to exercise restraint. This may well have been the reason why, at a very early age, some children were given the freedom to make decisions that would clearly be detrimental to their future. However, wherever it was possible to separate intention from practice, almost all parents from all walks of life would have liked to provide their children with the opportunities recommended by the Records. There were few, if any, who considered them irrelevant.

Furthermore, parents who do not meet these criteria do not fit neatly into any particular category. Parents who suffer from isolation may find it difficult to help their children to achieve a sense of self-esteem, but it is economic deprivation which has a greater effect on diet, and consequently health. Social class has little relevance when considered in isolation; separation and movement do not appear to be significant in themselves, as long as parents adopt strategies designed to mitigate their potential adverse effects. It is likely to be the interaction between a number of factors rather than any specific characteristic that leads to parenting difficulties. Thus most families are able to overcome adversities and provide their children with a sufficiently nurturing environment, although they may fall down in one or two areas. Only a very small proportion are unable to provide a sufficiently consistent standard of care across all seven dimensions, but it is they who form the group whose children are most likely to be admitted to care or accommodation. Because practitioners and carers generally only see children from this group, the criticism that the Assessment and Action Records promote values that are only acceptable to middle class families has arisen. If the purpose of looking after children away from home is to provide them with a standard of care that more closely approximates to that provided by parents in the community, then local authorities should expect to provide a service that meets the standard set by the Records.

The Records in themselves will not alleviate the multiple disadvantages suffered by many children in state care, but they can help to ensure that the children receive effective preventive health care; that they get the best possible education; that they have a realistic view of themselves and reasonable self-esteem. Family difficulties may have precipitated separation and exacerbated the emotional and behavioural difficulties of looked after children but we can still ensure that the children remain in touch with relatives (to whom most return) and receive specialist help for affective and conduct disorders. Similarly, children accommodated or in care deserve the support with social presentation and self care that is offered unconditionally by parents in most ordinary families.

Summary Points

1. Evidence from the community group suggests that almost all parents from all walks of life thought it important to provide their children with the opportunities recommended by the Records, although some were unable to do so. There were few, if any, who considered them irrelevant and, indeed, the recommended actions were widely regarded as a key to effective parenting.

2. Parents not meeting individual standards of effective parenting cannot be easily distinguished by characteristics such as social class, family structure, economic deprivation or isolation. It is likely to be the interaction between a number of factors rather than any specific characteristic that leads to parenting difficulties.

3. Most families in the community are able to overcome adversities and provide their children with a sufficiently nurturing environment, although they may fall down in one or two areas. Only a very small

proportion are unable to provide a sufficiently consistent standard of care across all seven dimensions.

4.   Ordinary parents have often learnt strategies to help children overcome difficulties which social services departments might find it useful to explore. Parents seemed relatively adept at helping their children cope with moving house or supporting them at school.

5.   However, the behaviour of parents in the community cannot be taken uncritically as a pattern to be followed by public bodies: a number of parents in our community group showed less concern for their children's safety or diet than one would expect to be offered to children in care or accommodation.

6.   The experience of the interviewers confirmed that the Assessment and Action Records can be used with parents and children in the community as a means of identifying difficulties and discussing how to address them. It was also relatively easy to identify children and young people whose multiple difficulties placed them at considerable risk.

Part Three

Implementing the
Assessment and Action
Records as part of a
comprehensive system for
planning and review

Chapter 5

Change in organisations: likely problems in implementing *Looking After Children*

Introduction

The research and development work described in this book has led to substantial revisions of the *Looking After Children* materials and the production of complementary publications, such as a training resources pack, a computer database and a management and implementation guide. Getting the instruments right was a considerable task but getting them into use raised a new set of issues. Although the extensive consultations with practitioners and carers revealed considerable interest in using the materials, we also came to understand the numerous obstacles that would have to be overcome if the full benefits of the system were to be reaped by local authorities.

In this chapter, the literature on organisational change is discussed in order to identify the implementation problems that might arise. These general observations are expanded in Chapter Six with messages from local authorities that have tried to introduce the Assessment and Action Records to social workers and carers and, in Chapter Seven, with a case study from one authority which has fully implemented *Looking After Children*. It is our hope that these implementation experiences will ease the process of introducing the materials in the 40 social services departments in England and Wales that have expressed an intention of implementing them.

The Context of Implementation

Barnardo and Stephenson, who pioneered child care services in the nineteenth century, would have seen no need to assess their contribution to welfare. To them, the benefits of separation and segregation and the rightness of their actions were self-evident. Parents who relinquished care were almost universally regarded as depraved and it was obvious that their children would only flourish if uprooted and transplanted to healthier, happier homes. The success of their experiment could be seen in the clean faces and new clothes that appear in Dr Barnardo's 'before and after' pictures, or in the meticulous inventories and menus drawn up to demonstrate the superiority of residential homes. Indeed, at a time when the clothing, housing and nutrition of the poorest families were blatantly inadequate, it is possible to argue that some children only survived through being looked after away from home.

However, a century later, the certainties that fired the nineteenth century philanthropists have all but disappeared. We no longer believe that the middle classes have a way of life that is self-evidently superior to that of their working class neighbours; nor, indeed, is there any longer a commonly-held assumption that one social group has the right or the duty to offer advice and examples which others will be expected meekly to follow. The blurring of an individual's social position and place in the order of society has been accompanied by increasing doubts about the role and status of those professions which once encapsulated the paternalistic function the middle classes were expected to fill.

All of this has put pressure on public services to be more answerable to clients, a development manifest in the publication of patient charters, the introduction of complaints procedures, the significance accorded to customers' views and the plethora of audits, inspections and reviews. Moreover, these same services face increasing threats of litigation and media exposure. Moves towards accountability, towards services that meet the needs of the consumer and offer good value for money, represent a major change in the values and assumptions that underpin professional practice. Thomas Kuhn (1970) would recognise this development of thinking as a 'paradigm shift' because change has occurred in the set of assumptions, theories and models that are commonly accepted and shared within a particular field of activity at any one point in time. The *Looking After Children* materials should be seen in this context: their development is symptomatic of the wider changes described and it is clear that had the original working party not fashioned the approaches we describe, some other group would have done so.

As well as this shift towards better assessment of needs and greater accountability of professionals, the context in which such assessments take place has also changed. The nineteenth century philanthropists had no doubt that deprived children should be placed either in residential or in foster homes that were headed by respectable, committed Christians. Christianity was seen not only as offering the children of depraved parents a hope of salvation, but also as providing the discipline and conformity to normative values that, in the interests of society in general, they were seen, most desperately, to need. But scientific evidence has cast doubt on the strengths of substitute care and over the last century religious belief has gradually been eroded. Christianity has long since ceased to be regarded as offering an effective means of social control; particularly in the last thirty years or so, as Britain has become a multi-cultural society, the assumption that the values of Christianity are, or at least should be, universally accepted has gone and they can no longer be assumed to provide the accepted value system for the upbringing of children.

The past few decades have also been accompanied by considerable social changes. Until very recently there was an implicit assumption that children needed to be brought up by two parents who were bound to one another by the contract of marriage. Over the last twenty years, the divorce rate has risen so that one in seven children are brought up in single parent families. Parallel to this trend is a rise in the number of parents who cohabit and have children outside marriage. In such a climate, illegitimacy has lost its stigma. It is now no longer universally accepted that children need to be brought up by two parents who have made a formal commitment to one another; indeed, single adults and gay couples are now being accepted as foster and adoptive parents and the outcomes of these arrangements are being seriously researched (Owen, forthcoming).

The loss of certainty that now characterises our assumptions about the nature of the family and the credibility of professionals is also apparent in our expectations of the child care service. The rigid severance policies which formed part of 'permanency planning' ideas in the 1970s and early '80s have been questioned. Increased interest in children's and family rights, together with a growing body of research emphasising the value of close relationships between looked after children and their natural families, have led central and local government policy makers to reflect on their priorities (Triseliotis, 1980; Millham *et al*, 1986; Bullock *et al*, 1993). The *Children Act 1989* emphasises the need to create and reinforce partnerships between natural parents, statutory agencies and all others who hold parental responsibility for children.

Although such policies are clearly in the interests of the children concerned, it is much more difficult for a statutory agency to share responsibilities with natural parents than simply to take over their role and provide permanent substitute homes. The part the state should play within such a relationship is by no means clear-cut and inevitably leads to questions about its aims and objectives and the extent of its authority. Should, for example, a statutory agency acknowledge that a parent with whom it shares responsibilities has a right to bring up a child according to a particular set of cultural values, or should it insist that the partnership depends on parents meeting the standard it sets?

In a climate of uncertainty, practitioners are not only likely to resist change, but will also resort to dogma and fashion, responses which can be exacerbated by inexperience or a lack of understanding. Several examples of rigid thinking can be found in local authority policies, such as the refusal to place any child under a certain age in a residential unit, regardless of individual circumstances, the insistence that all looked after children who fail to return to their parents within a certain time should be placed for adoption, or the acceptance of bizarre methods of control in residential units, based on perversions of the principles of behavioural therapy.

Looking After Children represents a sophisticated approach to meeting the needs of children. The Assessment and Action Records require professionals to take a broad perspective, looking at the child's needs in the areas of health, education and identity as well as living situations. They require professionals to review children's progress over time, to identify outstanding issues and to allocate responsibility to tackle them, thus linking assessment and planning. Carers and clients are involved in this process. If the materials are properly used, they encourage professionals to pick out problem cases, check standards, monitor competencies, undertake audits and judge services as a whole. The Records also produce aggregate data on an agency's work. The implications for social services departments implementing the system are, therefore, considerable.

The Process of Change in Organisations

Given that *Looking After Children* is part of a radical change in child care practice and maybe promises more upheaval, is it viable? Any development threatens vested interests but these new approaches to personal social services are particularly challenging to social work. Etzioni (1975) noted key differences between full professions, such as medicine and law and semi-professions, such as social work and teaching. The latter tend to have less autonomy and control by peers, practitioners are more bound up into bureaucracies and there are fewer organisational layers, meaning that promotion takes successful members out of practice and into management. As semi-professions are marked by low consensus among members about basic principles and a paucity of scientific evidence to justify practice, discussions about the implementation of the

Assessment and Action Records are likely to be lively as they encourage common standards based on sound research findings. They offer a method of developing practice but could well produce different levels of commitment from the various groups within a social services department.

The conditions for implementing the Assessment and Action Records were not, therefore, necessarily auspicious and there was a danger that, without a strategy to support their introduction into practice, all our efforts would be for nought. We were conscious that, while the *Children Act 1989* and other major reforms have effected a major shift in thinking, the history of child care is littered with other examples of minute adjustments to existing practice which have had only cosmetic effect. For example, every morning boys in one approved school lined up each in number order in a decaying wooden building called the drill hall. After the community homes reforms of the early 1970s, boys still lined up in the same way, but the Nissen hut was now called the forum.

Hall, Land, Parker and Webb (1975) constructed a model to explain why some ideas achieve cogency, become a social issue and get adopted as policy while others do not. Initially, they considered three levels of change: initiation which involves new ventures for an agency, development which changes the scale of existing activity and reform which recasts policies within those spheres of activity. Implementation of the Assessment and Action Records is most certainly the last of the three types of change in that it provides a new way of practice but it also involves some change of scale within the continuity of child care work. It is not, however, a major policy shift that forms part of a political agenda. There are no trade unions to be convinced and no party manifestos are under threat. As the model postulates that the less radical the change the more likely it is to occur, there is some scope for optimism about the implementation possibilities of *Looking After Children*.

The model outlined by Hall and her colleagues goes on to specify the criteria for likely adoption by policy makers. It asks, firstly, whether the proposals are legitimate in that people think the agency should be involved and, secondly, whether they are feasible in terms of knowledge, technology, resources, collaboration between groups and administrative capacity. With regard to *Looking After Children*, the answer to the second question is much clearer than the first. The Assessment and Action Records are based on sound scientific evidence, key people, such as the Social Services Inspectorate and Department of Health ministers and policy makers, acknowledge their value and there is general support from the professional associations representing social workers, foster carers, families and children.

The answer to the first question on legitimacy is more equivocal. Government, whether central or local, has legal responsibilities to provide high quality social services, but telling professionals how to do their job is arguably beyond its remit. In medicine and law, professional autonomy is respected even if, as some commentators claim, it has been eroded somewhat in recent years. Thus, the policy question of whether the Assessment and Action Records should become widely used or even be made mandatory has wider political implications and the view that they represent an undue interference by Government could hinder implementation, irrespective of their intrinsic worth.

Hall and her colleagues go on to list the factors which influence the image of an issue and its likely acceptance, some of which augur particularly well for the Assessment and Action Records. They provide extensive and reliable information for a service undertaking difficult work, they help professionals prevent and tackle crises, they relate diverse issues within an overarching concept of welfare and they are generally viewed by professionals as being significantly better than most recording systems in use. Balanced against these benefits are the facts that the Records are not essential to the resolution of pressing disputes and that child care agencies would not be seriously disadvantaged if they ignored them altogether. It is also the case that the initiative has come mostly from the Department of Health and may therefore be seen by potential users as serving

Government needs rather than their own. Indeed, some cynics may suggest that they represent the thin end of the wedge with regard to the central control of local social services' activities and scrutiny of their use of resources. Nevertheless, as over half of the factors cited by Hall and her colleagues suggest a successful implementation, there is room for optimism.

A weakness of the approach just described is its failure to distinguish between technical improvements by which welfare aims are pursued and changes that affect the aims themselves. The Assessment and Action Records do both. They are a better practice tool but, at the same time, incorporate a particular concept of what services should be and how they should be provided. But despite these useful qualities, it must be acknowledged that professionals' suspicions of a hidden agenda are likely to generate considerable discussion.

In deciding how best to introduce the Assessment and Action Records into local authorities, we also drew upon lessons from case studies of organisational change both in public services and commercial enterprises. Such studies tend to question the value of general models of change like those outlined by Hall and colleagues. Pettigrew and Whipp (1991), for example, doubt the existence of universal 'laws' in this area and instead propose a set of inter-related factors which, they argue, must be considered and managed during the change process.

They and many other researchers highlight the significance of the context in which change is sought and the factors peculiar to each situation. For instance, they show how the timing of new developments and the climate at the time of their introduction have to be right if good intentions are not to be frustrated. Compare, for example, the short-lived introduction of unitary fines brought about by the *Criminal Justice Act 1991* with the more enduring success of the *Education Act 1981*. In the former, despite an entirely rational plan to keep fine defaulters out of prison and relate punishments to people's ability to pay, public opinion was dramatically swayed by media reports of cases where the levels of fines were extreme, calling the justice system into disrepute. The legislation was repealed, despite research evidence that means-testing is still used by many courts considering what penalties to impose.

In contrast, a different set of circumstances surrounded the implementation of the *Education Act 1981*. Policy strands, such as the closure of some special schools and professional views on the needs of children with learning and behavioural difficulties, came together simultaneously, aided by demographic changes which reduced the demand for boarding places. The legislation was generally viewed as a great success and marked a significant shift towards better mainstream services for children with educational and behavioural difficulties. When considering change, all the factors that could influence the development of policy have to be taken into account if the process is to be understood.

The Local Child Care Context

The national context and changes within the social work profession as a whole have already been discussed. But, if the local context is considered, different questions arise about the chances of the materials being widely used by social services departments. Within local authorities three types of problem seem likely: organisational, attitudinal and ideological.

All bureaucracies are marked by some degree of conservatism among middle management. Social services are a typical, but not necessarily an extreme case; indeed, they deserve credit for implementing many child care reforms over the last 30 years. Nevertheless, the considerable expansion and the level of funding they have enjoyed compared with some other local government departments, such as housing, since their creation in 1971 have not reduced the inherent fear of change. The Assessment and Action Records provide staff with something to be resisted, an attractive and functional role for overworked people facing uncertainty.

It was suggested earlier in this chapter that staff may be suspicious of the motives that lie behind a system as comprehensive as *Looking After Children*. In addition to increasing control, recent experience of changes in community care has led some social workers to be wary of demands for clearer role definitions, particularly those which delineate core professional tasks so that the remaining work can be delegated to staff who are less qualified. Such developments can already be seen in medicine, teaching and the police. The use of set questionnaires with accompanying guidance could be perceived as potentially undermining child care professionalism by suggesting that 'anyone can do it'. These anxieties will be especially high in a context where future administrative frameworks and local government structures are uncertain. In such a situation, a less than enthusiastic response to implementation is likely.

Another difficulty is that top-down directives are generally unpopular in local social services. As Packman and Hall (1995) have shown, social workers have been the recipients of seemingly endless rounds of organisational change orchestrated by local management. All this has had to be accomplished on top of recent children's and community care legislation and the proposed establishment of unitary authorities. 'They're sea sick with change,' said one assistant director, 'they already have 33 forms on children to complete and they'll really need persuading of the benefits of filling up more.' An inherent problem in constructing materials designed to gather information or to act as guides to assessment and planning is that it is almost impossible to avoid creating them in the form of questionnaires; the Assessment and Action Records inevitably increase the amount of paperwork practitioners are required to complete.

Much of the preparation prior to the implementation of *Looking After Children* served to remind professionals that the materials are no more than tools; completing an Assessment and Action Record is not a substitute for action, but a framework for good practice. It is not intended as a bureaucratic, form-filling exercise and, indeed, it will be of little value if it is used as such. The materials will only be useful if they serve the practitioner; those who regard the object of the exercise as being to complete the forms rather than to involve children, young people, parents, carers and others in the planning and assessment process have misunderstood their function.

The preliminary work also suggested that expressed objections to using the Assessment and Action Records frequently mask other concerns. The most common complaints from practitioners have been about a lack of resources and a perception that the Records undermine professional autonomy. Yet these concerns have little justification. Feasibility studies show that few extra resources are needed to administer *Looking After Children* and it is very unlikely that major decisions about the care of children separated from home would ever be delegated to unqualified staff. Although persuasion and argument should be sufficient to satisfy practitioners, opinions are likely to be deeply held.

One of the major difficulties to overcome is the fact that the culture of social work practice emphasises the importance of individual cases and puts a premium on interactive talk and action rather than seeking generalities, recording and evaluation. Rigid classifications of clients are generally disliked by social workers and some are wary of the possible political and professional misuse of typologies — 'the unintended consequences of intended human action'. There could be underlying fears that the information produced by the Assessment and Action Records might be used to identify potential delinquents among six-year-olds, to judge parents' competence before their child is born or to produce crude league tables showing the quality of services in different local authorities.

In summary, unless it can be demonstrated that social work intervention will deteriorate without the implementation of *Looking After Children*, some resistance from users is inevitable; indeed, such responses could be highly functional for over-worked staff dealing directly with children and families. Various studies of field and residential social workers have emphasised the need for professionals to feel in control and to believe that their contribution makes a difference (Howe, 1986; Baldwin, 1990), despite the fact that they actually had much more power than they realised (Vernon and Fruin, 1986).

The plans for implementing *Looking After Children* have taken these factors into account. Local authorities are being encouraged to introduce the materials slowly, for example, by using selected groups who are willing to experiment and in a way that allows professionals time for reflection. Hasty implementation would be counter-productive and practitioners need to see that they are not under attack. They must not be made to feel that they are being viewed as ineffective.

The Conditions for Successful Implementation

What other messages have been drawn from the preceding discussion about the best way of implementing *Looking After Children*? The experts on organisational change give one set of advice. Kuhn (1970) writes, 'a well developed paradigm, or a strong culture, is overturned with great difficulty, even if it fails to account for data or lead to new discoveries.' 'In a similar fashion', writes Janis (1972), 'an organisational paradigm provides a way of thinking about and investigating the world, which reduces uncertainty and provides for collective effective action, but which also overlooks or ignores certain lines of inquiry. It is easy for a strong culture to produce groupthink, a pressure to conform to the dominant view'. Peters (1982) is more to the point but no more optimistic. 'To be successful and stay in business, organisations need not only to cope with change but to thrive on it.' Clearly, there is a need to encourage local authorities to develop a culture which values the results of using the Assessment and Action Records, such as good monitoring, a focus on the whole child, outcome evidence, access to high quality aggregate data and the other benefits described in this book.

Management literature indicates other factors that should facilitate successful implementation of the materials. It stresses the interrelationship between the parts of organisations and the fact that members also participate in occupational and political sub-systems. As the co-operation of every social worker is being sought for *Looking After Children*, a participatory model of implementation, which emphasises the process of change rather than relying on directives from senior managers, is more likely to succeed. However, as Johnson (1988) suggests, the likelihood of professionals complying with the changes being introduced will depend not so much on the intellectual case made for the approach or on the application of overt rewards and sanctions as on the degree to which the changes produce demonstrable improvements in services.

In planning the implementation of *Looking After Children* we also drew on the work of Pettigrew and Whipp (1991), whose study of National Health Service reforms provides several rules for managing change successfully. An adequate appreciation of the context in which social services departments operate is clearly important. With regard to *Looking After Children*, those local authorities that are most aware of recent developments in social work and public service have been the first to appreciate fully the potential of the material and have been the most receptive to its implementation. An irony, however, has been that these agencies have also been the most likely to have an effective monitoring and evaluation system already in place.

Naturally, leadership has an influence on the levels of commitment to the project. Most change in organisations is incremental rather than dramatic and usually involves wide consultation. The main task of leaders is to create a receptive climate and to provide encouragement and support early on. Some organisational changes need a charismatic leader, others a tough manager, but the implementation of *Looking After Children* requires neither; experience from the evaluation study suggests it is more likely to benefit from concern, vision, persuasion and staying power.

Two other factors help explain the receptivity of an organisation to the type of change being introduced. The first is the extent to which there are key personnel who are prepared to champion new techniques. The Assessment and Action Records require agencies to be responsive to ideas from outside and to involve carers, families and children in the care process. Managers have to be willing to learn from staff and staff have to be prepared to learn from clients. The second condition is the degree to which the assessments are part of a multi-functional activity, not pursued as an end in itself but as an integral part of the organisation's day to day operation. This echoes Peters' (1982) emphasis on an inquisitive and developmental culture discussed earlier in this chapter.

As a general conclusion, the research literature on organisational change indicates that the best way of achieving successful implementation of the Assessment and Action Records is to build on social workers' and carers' perceptions of their task rather than to demolish existing practices and seek radical alteration. Social workers often express the need to work in partnership with clients with the aim of achieving modest improvements in the situation of vulnerable families. Social work, like the Records, aims to promote welfare and we have stressed this common purpose in trying to get them used. We have also encouraged individual practitioners to consider what using the Records means for them and for their clients in the hope that they will see the system as a valuable aid to professional work rather than as a check on their activity or an imposed chore. As the following chapters demonstrate, this approach won wide approval for the project among practitioners.

Howe (1986) concluded his study of field social workers by outlining ways in which change has been successfully introduced into social services. Learning from developments in professional fostering schemes for difficult teenagers and from attempts to provide community care for the frail elderly, he argues that there is a need to be open and informed and to encourage professionals to understand precisely what is being sought and the reasons for introducing the change. Local authorities introducing *Looking After Children* have therefore been encouraged to recognise the special skills of their workers and to show how these are enhanced by using the Records. One long-standing social work maxim is 'start where the client is', a view easily applied to the Assessment and Action Records by virtue of their design.

Conclusion

This chapter has explored the context in which *Looking After Children* has been developed and the factors that indicate the success or otherwise of its implementation. The messages are mixed. At a national level, child care services are moving towards a professionalism that requires authoritative data underpinned by research. As the proposed changes are neither too radical nor part of a wider political agenda, the adoption of the system, or something very similar to it, seems almost essential. The benefits for the child care services, for social workers, carers and clients, are clear.

At the local level, the situation is more problematic. Despite a lot of goodwill, practical obstacles seem considerable. Some are natural responses to perceived upheaval, others stem from ideological questions and concerns about government inter- ference in professional matters. Motivation is a major problem. At present, there is no onus on agencies to revise their monitoring methods and little accountability if their system is unsatisfactory. It has been argued that this could be a short- sighted and dangerous view.

In the longer term, it is almost inevitable that the ideas that underpin *Looking After Children* will influence practice in all child care agencies. But this is not the end of the process. In time, the ideas and their application in the materials will date. The large scale social engineering programmes of the 1960s, such as the Educational Priority Areas and Community Development Programmes, left a valuable legacy of practice but one which seemed to stifle intellectual debate. As a result, the ideas of Halsey, Titmuss and others that inspired the original projects are still those which stimulate researchers even though the context in which such ideas are applied is now markedly different. It has to be said of the 1960s projects that equal academic benefit would have been obtained from a smaller practical exercise. The large-scale implementation and demonstration projects did not enhance the theoretical ideas as much as had been hoped.

The same thing could happen to the more modest endeavours of *Looking After Children*. The concern with implementation has tended to divert attention from the concept of outcome, the focus of the original working party. Most subsequent discussions with practitioners has focused on the viability and content of the Assessment and Action Records and associated Planning and Review forms. While it is important that *Looking After Children* should be widely used, it is equally important to get practitioners to engage with the idea of child care outcomes. This intellectual leap is necessary in order to maintain the impetus of the project. Hopefully, theoretical ideas will be developed further once the current round of implementation is completed.

Finally, it is inevitable that there will be some counter-reaction to the current quest for rationality in social work thinking. *Looking After Children* will come under close scrutiny as values change and prevailing ideas are criticised. Tensions and debates can be healthy features of organisations, leading to clearer policies and greater efficiency. It is important to realise that the service model which the Assessment and Action Records support is ephemeral as are the criteria for evaluating outcomes. Particularly significant in future discussions will be cost/benefit studies of children's care careers and packages of care services.

All in all, the present context for introducing *Looking After Children* seems favourable. Pressures from audit, inspection, media and courts demand sophisticated evidence and child care services will have to respond accordingly. The culture of the personal social services seems amenable to change and the methods most likely to achieve success have been described. The *Looking After Children* materials have been welcomed when they are seen to build on and develop the best elements of child care practice. The ideological obstacles are harder to forecast and reflect the perennial tension between research and practice. Until this lessens, the practitioners whom the system is designed to help will inevitably be somewhat sceptical about its alleged benefits.

The value that social workers place on the types of information produced by the Assessment and Action Records is a key variable identified in this chapter. Do they feel that the effort of gathering all the data is worthwhile? Do they feel the client's view is useful? The general hypothesis suggested by this and other studies predicts that the greater the gap between the ideas that underpin the system and the practicality of collecting the information, the greater will be the resistance. Change is always difficult to bring about in 'belief' areas because motivations have to come from within. *Looking After Children* is both a technical innovation and a proponent of a particular care philosophy. It is precisely because it has set its aims wide that it is likely to meet some difficulties in its implementation.

Summary Points

1. The concern with child care outcomes reflects recent moves towards a needs-led service and the increasing accountability of professionals to clients.

2. In a situation where there is uncertainty about the best context in which to rear children, the role and responsibilities of statutory agencies which share parenting responsibilities with families will be ambiguous.

3. As many front-line carers have limited experience in looking after children, practice tools which raise key issues and offer guidance will be useful.

4. *Looking After Children* fulfils several important functions for an agency caring for young people separated from home. These will be increasingly valuable, given the ways in which personal social services are developing.

5. Messages from studies of organisational change indicate that the implementation of *Looking After Children* is viable provided that problems arising from the structure of bureaucracies, the attitudes of staff and the ideology of social work are addressed.

6. The factors likely to lead to successful implementation are: sensitivity to the context in which services for children and families are provided, good leadership, the willingness of staff to entertain ideas from outside and awareness of likely sources of dissatisfaction.

7. Successful implementation is most likely to be achieved by acknowledging the skills of professionals and demonstrating to them the benefits of the project for policy and practice.

Chapter 6

Research messages for implementation

Introduction

When, in 1991, we asked four local authorities to use the Assessment and Action Records to scrutinise the experiences and progress of a study group of looked after children, the possibility of their being implemented throughout an authority had not yet been raised. The Records were originally conceived as research tools and we were still expecting that they would be used for small groups of children, possibly as part of an inspection procedure. The reader therefore needs to bear in mind that the four participating local authorities agreed to conduct a time-limited research exercise; as a result, although the information obtained conveys messages which are useful in considering implementation, that was not the original focus of the study.

Will Anybody Use the Assessment and Action Records?

It will be recalled that the four local authorities were each invited to assess 50 children in order to provide a looked after study group, constructed in order to explore the use of the Assessment and Action Records in various settings. (The fifth authority, E, was not involved in this part of the research and will not be included in the following discussion). The primary research question asked at this stage was simply whether it would be possible to persuade social workers to provide this relatively large number of assessments.

There were grounds for this concern because the response from the preliminary trials had been uneven, despite the fact that far fewer assessments had then been required. Moreover those assessments had been completed by hand-picked volunteers; in the evaluation study described in this book, most participants were involved because of a management decision to use the materials, and had little choice as to whether or not they would participate. We also initially had some difficulty in persuading local authorities to agree to such a large number of assessments. In the event, after negotiation, only two agreed to assess the full quota of 50 children. We eventually made arrangements for the two other authorities to participate on condition that they each assessed a minimum of 30 cases.

In spite of this rather discouraging beginning, as we showed in Chapter Two, two authorities produced considerably more than their agreed quota of assessments, while only one failed to meet its target. The two most responsive authorities are both continuing to use the Records to assess the experiences and progress of all their looked after children.

One reason why the number of completed assessments exceeded our expectations was that social workers proved to be more enthusiastic about undertaking the work than had been anticipated; it seems probable that the extensive training that most social services departments provided to accompany the implementation of the *Children Act 1989* was responsible for the change of climate. Moreover, a requirement to evaluate the effectiveness of a service is increasingly accepted as normal practice in numerous public and private institutions, and it no longer seemed so alien to social workers.

However, although the results confirm that there was considerable enthusiasm for the undertaking, it should be noted that this was only sustained under certain circumstances. As the preliminary trials had already indicated, participants were more likely to complete assessments if the project had the unequivocal support of management, if there were clear, attainable timescales, if there was a specific requirement for all staff in a team or area office to take part and if a researcher was available to help when difficulties arose. This was confirmed in one authority where all social workers in one area team agreed to scrutinise a sample of children and young people over the age of ten within a six week period. The researcher trained the social workers in the use of the materials, and fed back the results of the exercise to them, but it was the team manager who encouraged his staff to participate, and made sure that all the assessments were completed on time. It is also noteworthy that this group had a high level of support from administrative staff. This team assessed its agreed quota of 30 teenagers and young people, and repeated the process with them all a year later, without any apparent difficulties.

Not all the local authorities succeeded in sustaining the attention of participants to the same extent. In another authority the researcher worked closely with the family placement officer who selected a sample of 30 children who were either in residential care or who had experienced difficulties settling in foster homes. Again the exercise was well received: staff offered to assess all the children living in some of the residential units visited by the researcher, although only two or three had officially been selected for the study group. It proved, however, much harder than expected for residential staff to find the time and space to undertake the work and, even with the support of a researcher, a smaller number of additional assessments was produced than had been anticipated. Nevertheless, use of the materials gradually spread to other areas of the authority.

In all participating authorities, the exercise was valued as providing an experience that would benefit social workers, carers and the children for whom they shared responsibilities. It seems unlikely that social services departments will need much encouragement to use the Assessment and Action Records to undertake specific exercises such as these, and indeed we know that this is being done already, outside the aegis of the research project.

The Extent to Which the Assessment and Action Records Were Completed

However, the exercise will have little value unless it is done properly. Once we had resolved the initial question of whether anyone would ever use the Records, we were concerned to discover how thoroughly participants completed the assessments and how far they had used the materials as we had intended.

The results from the current study show that almost all the primary 'quality of care' questions were answered. Social workers and carers were willing to examine the everyday details of the children's experiences, and claimed to have learned a great deal from doing so. We cannot tell how truthful the responses were, but many respondents admitted to deficiencies at least in some areas of care, and most identified instances where important information about a child was unavailable. In the words of one social worker, the assessments were 'very useful and exacting. The deficits in our information are glaring'.

There were, however, three instances in which the primary 'quality of care' questions were ignored. Firstly, Chapter Three has already indicated that social workers did not always consider it necessary to answer questions on identity if a child were white, even though only a few of these refer to racial issues, and the dimension covers many other areas that are relevant to all looked after children.

Secondly, the questions in the education section were occasionally disregarded if the child were one of the 10% in the looked after group who were not attending school. This appears to be a contentious issue: a reasonable parent might consider it his or her responsibility to try to compensate for a period out of school by offering additional help with a child's education. It certainly seems odd that practitioners with some parental responsibilities considered it irrelevant to explore a child's educational experiences during a break in schooling. If it does nothing else, a string of negative responses to the education questions serves to demonstrate how much a child loses when excluded from formal education, particularly when there is no-one who regards it as their responsibility to try to take compensatory action.

Thirdly, a small group of respondents attempted to complete the first few questions, and then gave up. It was clear from other evidence — not least the comments on some of the questions — that these Records had been handed to young people to complete in isolation, with no assistance from carers or social workers. Most of them had neither the power of concentration nor the literacy skills to do more than begin the exercise. One of the key messages of the project is that assessments should be used as a basis for making plans to improve the quality of care that children receive; clearly this can only be achieved if they are undertaken as joint exercises in which all those responsible participate. The *Children Act 1989* emphasises the importance of creating and sustaining partnerships between children, parents, carers, social workers and other professionals; when used as intended, the Assessment and Action Records can help in this respect. Assessments undertaken in isolation are of little value and should be discouraged.

Responses to the Questions About Aims

The Assessment and Action Records first ask participants whether certain parental actions have been undertaken, and then require them to assess how far children have progressed towards the goals to which they relate. Apart from the instances noted above, the questions about parental care, or inputs, were generally answered satisfactorily; however, those about the achievement of goals, or outcomes, were not. Participants were asked to answer these questions by discussing with one another what the response should be, and then indicating each child's position on an unmarked linear scale. (An example of the scale is shown in the demonstration section from the original Record in Appendix Two). However, many practitioners found the exercise confusing and produced invalid responses; others ignored these questions, left the scales blank or needed further advice before completing them. Many respondents failed to appreciate that the scales were all of a standard length and would provide quantifiable data about children's progress over time. Very few gave details of disagreements, although invited to do so.

It is unfortunate that this proved the most difficult part of the Records to complete, for these questions about aims are intended to encourage respondents to gather information about children's progress as it relates to the quality of care they have received and thus to consider the question of outcome. If social workers are to appreciate the value of the Records as assessment and planning tools, they need to appreciate the ideas behind them. The hypothesis that there is a causal link between parenting inputs and long-term outcomes is widely accepted, but it needs to be openly articulated and debated. All parents, for instance, are aware that they need to provide their children with adequate food if they are to grow; those who look after children away from home need to accept that the failures of corporate parenting identified by numerous research studies can similarly affect outcome. The Records provide practitioners and carers with up-to-date research information about effective parenting, but many issues are still a matter for debate. In many instances the link between a particular practice and a specific outcome is assumed rather than proved; there are also questions to be asked about the standards, priorities and limitations that an agency should regard as acceptable. Until practitioners begin to engage in this debate, the potential of the Records to influence and improve corporate parenting will not be fully exploited.

We have begun to address this issue by removing the practical obstacles that may have obscured the link between input and outcome. The revised version of the Assessment and Action Records gives greater prominence to the assessments of objectives, abandons the unmarked linear scales in favour of more specific, graded responses, and provides clearer guidance on the way in which they should be completed. It still remains possible that this part of the Records will not be properly completed until practitioners have a greater appreciation of the value of the data collected. Although the *Looking After*

114

Children Management and Implementation Guide which accompanies the revised materials emphasises the significance of these data, front-line workers are unlikely to give sufficient attention to these assessments without encouragement from supervisors and managers.

Further Training

Some of the difficulties encountered by those who completed the Records have been addressed in the revised version; most problems indicate a need for further training rather than any major deficits in the materials. Issues such as how far the Records should be used as discussion documents, whether teenagers should ever be encouraged to fill them in on their own and how the assessments of objectives should be approached are specific to the implementation of the system and are dealt with in the *Looking After Children Training Resources Pack*. This pack also includes a reader, designed to reinforce the research messages about issues of importance to outcomes for looked after children covered by the questions on the Records. Other broader anomalies, such as the reluctance of some social workers to consider issues surrounding the establishment of identity or the promotion of education for looked after children, indicate the need for a greater debate about the standards which local authorities should seek to attain and should be addressed as part of general social work training.

Using the Assessment and Action Records on a Regular Basis

The evidence shows that, with support, social workers and carers will use the Assessment and Action Records as a practice tool that facilitates discussion about outcomes. However, although the Records can and do stand alone, it was one of the fundamental principles of the original working party that outcomes need to be viewed not as isolated instances, but as sequences of events that should be regularly monitored as part of everyday social work practice because 'looked at against what went before and compared with what follows next an 'outcome' may seem neither as bad nor as good as it did when regarded as a solitary episode' (Parker *et al*, 1991).

In order to find out the likelihood of the Assessment and Action Records being used on a regular basis, social workers in the current study were asked to assess children in the looked after group on two occasions, separated by an interval of a year. As Table 6.1 shows, most authorities experienced greater difficulties in assessing children on the second occasion than they had on the first.

Table 6.1: *Second Assessments in the Looked After Group*

Authority	Number of Second Assessments Expected	Number of Second Assessments Produced
Authority A	30	30
Authority B	50	26
Authority C	36	19
Authority D	38	8
TOTAL	154	83

Problems were greatest in Authority D, which completed only a fifth of the expected number of second assessments. Here a major reorganisation during the evaluation period entailed the reconstitution of social work teams, the transfer of staff between area offices and the reallocation of cases. Social workers who moved to new positions or took over new caseloads felt little commitment to complete an exercise in which they had not previously been involved. Since *Looking After Children* began, we have seen similar reorganisations in about a third of the local authorities in which we have been working. On every occasion the disruption has placed serious obstacles in the way of developing long-term strategies for children's services, a point that has also been noted by other researchers (Packman and Hall, 1995).

The other authorities avoided similar upheavals, but two of them still struggled to complete a full quota of assessments. In Authorities B and C, just under half the children were regarded as ineligible for a second assessment as a year into the project they had either moved away from the participating area office or had left the care of the local authority altogether. In Authority C, two of the five residential units originally participating in the study had been closed for refurbishment and their children scattered around the authority by the time second assessments were due; 25 of the original 36 children from this authority changed placements during the research period. In both these authorities children's movement appeared to have been a much greater factor in preventing follow-up assessments than a lack of commitment from carers and social workers.

Although the movement of children and social workers may be a respectable reason for discontinuing participation in a research study, it is, to say the least, questionable whether this should be a reason for opting out of follow-up assessments when the Records are used as a part of everyday practice, and there are serious implications here for implementation. It is disappointing to find that social workers considered that they had no responsibility to undertake follow-up assessments of children and young people who had left the care of the local authority even when, as in some cases, they were adolescents who had 'moved to independent living'. Although it is to be hoped that implementation throughout a local authority would mean that the responsibility for follow-up assessments would be transferred when children or social workers moved, it increasingly emerged that without clear guidance and super-vision, this may be difficult to achieve. Certainly, if the Assessment and Action Records are to be completed on a regular basis there needs to be an authority-wide policy about how they should be used, and who should be responsible for seeing that they are filled in. A major advantage of implement-ing such a policy would be to ensure some continuity in the quality of care that children receive, and to monitor their progress wherever they are placed.

Although the evaluation study has produced little evidence of resistance to the work from social workers and carers, it would be unwise to draw the conclusion that this will not occur. In only one authority were respondents asked to assess all the children for whom they were responsible; most of those involved had agreed to participate on the understanding that the study was time-limited, and that they would only be asked to assess one or two children on a couple of occasions. Caseload management will be of particular importance to authorities considering implementation: in generic teams, a few social workers will often deal with a disproportionate number of child care cases; such cases will need to be carefully allocated if social workers are not to rush through the Records, ignoring the messages they bring in the desire to finish them as quickly as possible. One social worker we found completing the Records alone in her office, complaining that 'I might have been working with the children instead of wasting my time filling in these' offered an example of how the purpose of the assessments can be misunderstood when pressures of work reduce the opportunities for reflection.

Making Plans

A cogent reason for arguing that assessments of outcome should be undertaken at regular intervals was to encourage social workers to use the information collected in making plans to improve the quality of children's experiences. When shortfalls are identified, the Records therefore require respondents to record plans for further, remedial action and to identify who will be responsible for carrying them out, or else to give reasons for decisions to do nothing.

Evidence from 83 children who were assessed twice indicates that, where actions that are widely recognised as important were found to have been overlooked, effective remedial action was often taken. All but one of the children who could not explain why they were not living at home at the first assessment

118

could do so a year later; almost half of those who had been prescribed glasses but were not wearing them were doing so by the time of the second assessment. Changes had been slower where actions were considered of less importance to children's development. For instance, the question of whether children should be encouraged to go on school trips proved to be a contentious issue; although trips can promote children's social development as well as their academic progress, they are often perceived as an unwelcome and perhaps unnecessary expense. Just over one in three of the children in the looked after group had missed a school trip in the year preceding the first assessment; in only one instance was there clear evidence of plans being made to take remedial action, and by the second assessment two thirds of these children were still missing out.

We have already indicated that a high proportion of children were not assessed on a second occasion because they moved placement. Where practitioners had succeeded in following up children who had moved, some attempts were made to ensure that a consistent standard of care was maintained from one placement to the next, although these were not always successful. Children who moved during the assessment period were as likely to have their statutory medicals and immunisations as those who remained in the same placement. However, they were less likely to belong to clubs or to regard themselves as being good at anything; they had fewer friends outside the care system and they were more likely to smoke. It is difficult to distinguish between cause and effect, and some of these experiences may have influenced the decision to change placement; nevertheless, the disruption caused by moves will undoubtedly have been contributory to these adverse outcomes. The advantages of using the Assessment and Action Records as a means of keeping track of plans and thereby reducing some of the disruption were evident. It also seems probable that regular use of the Records will make it easier to identify at an early stage those children who are becoming dislocated from community and social networks.

The Role of the Supervisor

While we found little resistance to using the Assessment and Action Records as discussion documents, respondents did not always appreciate how they could be used as a basis for planning improvements to the quality of care that children receive. We found, for instance, a residential unit in which there was a policy to complete an Assessment and Action Record with each young person as soon as they arrived. An interview with one of the young people concerned confirmed that this had been appreciated as a valuable means of enabling a key worker to build up a relationship that went beyond 'the two of us sitting on either side of the fire wondering what to say to one another'. However, there had been no attempt to act on the information gathered: the completed Record had been handed to the young person and hidden in a drawer and forgotten. It seems likely that instances such as the above will be widespread unless the Records are introduced into the regular process of supervision and review. It is also probable that without the prompts provided by a supervisor, they will only be used haphazardly; we already know that without arrangements for disinterested monitoring, assessments and reviews can easily be overlooked or skimped (Sinclair, 1984).

Although the key role of the supervisor will be to check that the planning process is functioning adequately, he or she should also be ready to identify anomalies revealed by the assessment. It is to be hoped, for instance, that a supervisor would have questioned the plan to 'work towards adoption with current carers' for one child in the looked after group who had a poor relationship with all members of the placement family and whose foster carer 'had to make a conscious effort to show her physical affection.'

The Records all conclude with a summary of future work, designed to draw together the detailed plans that are made as each section is completed, and to be scrutinised at each review. The authority which had the least investment in the research was the one where staff paid least attention to summarising plans for future work; those authorities where team leaders were closely supervising the completion of the assessments were those where the summaries were most likely to be filled in adequately.

A Comprehensive System for Planning and Review

Much of the evidence described in this chapter points towards the importance of the Assessment and Action Records being set within frameworks for the planning and review of looked after children. In anticipation of this, the original working party had produced Basic Facts Sheets, Plans and Review Forms to demonstrate how the Records might be used within the statutory reviewing system. The use of these forms was not part of the original research project, but when it became clear that they held the key to successful implementation, further work on their development was undertaken in order to ensure that they formed a comprehensive and acceptable structure through which the Assessment and Action Records might be introduced.

There were other reasons for looking more closely at these Planning and Review forms. The *Children Act 1989* had been accompanied by detailed guidance and regulations for making plans and reviewing arrangements for children's cases (Department of Health, 1991c): a number of local authorities, faced with the time-consuming and complex task of devising written materials that met these new requirements, began to use these forms as though they were an official blueprint. Thus this, initially subsidiary, part of the project was thrust into an unexpected prominence that required the materials to be formally assessed, revised and piloted.

The reconstruction of the Planning and Review forms required exceptionally close co-operation between policy makers, practitioners and researchers, all of whom viewed the task from different perspectives. Policy makers needed materials that met the extremely intricate requirements of the law, the representatives from local authorities wanted to alert practitioners to these requirements, but also needed instruments that would be of practical use. The researchers' role was to translate these requirements into practical documents that reflected the principles that underpin *Looking After Children.*

Some issues needed careful negotiation; for instance, although it is quite clearly in their best interests to make careful plans before they are looked after, we know that a high proportion of children and young people who are well-known to social services departments are placed in an emergency. There was a strong temptation to produce materials that discouraged the use of unplanned placements, yet to do so would have alienated the social workers who completed them. We compromised by producing documents that could easily be used in emergencies, but that emphasised the principle that the majority of the work should be completed after careful consultation with all parties concerned.

Design was a key consideration, for it was necessary to produce materials that were attractive to users, but that could also be photocopied; that covered the requirements of the law and good practice, but that did not appear too lengthy; and that explained the purpose of some of the questions, without seeming patronising or overbearing. The fundamental require-ment was to produce materials that would be properly used; this part of the project benefited greatly from the advice of practitioners and their managers, several of whom were directly involved in the development work.

The *Arrangements for Placement of Children Regulations (1991)* require responsible authorities to draw up a plan in writing for any child whom they propose to look after or accommodate; the *Review of Children's Cases Regulations (1991)* require them to review the cases of all looked after children at statutory intervals. The original Plan and Review Form were designed to meet the detailed requirements specified in these regulations. However, the feedback showed that, although legally acceptable, the originals failed to meet the practical requirements of users. The Plan made no clear distinction between the long-term objectives of the admission, and the day-to-day provisions to be asked of carers. This ambiguity meant that a new Plan had to be drawn up whenever a child changed placement, a factor that counteracted the aim of preserving some continuity of objective throughout a child's care career. We were also advised that a number of the issues covered by the original Plan should more properly be considered as part of a Placement Agreement.

The revised materials answer these criticisms and place the Records in the context of a comprehensive planning and reviewing system for local authorities. Long-term objectives for children are agreed and monitored through the Care Plan and the Review Form, while short-term arrangements are made through the Placement Plan, of which the first part is the formal Placement Agreement. The Review Form was regarded as giving too little prominence to the views of children and young people, their parents and their carers: Consultation Papers have since been produced to help them put forward their points of view when faced with a meeting which can appear to be dominated by more articulate professionals. Thus, all the original forms have been radically revised with the intention of offering a clear structure within which public bodies can reproduce the planning and monitoring processes that parents routinely undertake as a matter of course, albeit less formally and systematically.

Throughout the evaluation study we have been aware that a major problem for looked after children has been the ease with which earlier plans and objectives can be abandoned when a new social worker arrives on the scene, or a new placement is made. If they do nothing else, the data from our looked after group should demonstrate how urgently these children need a sense of long-term stability. The new documentation emphasises that it should not be possible to alter the long-term plans for a child outside a formal review meeting: if an urgent need to reconsider the aims and objectives of the intervention arises, then those responsible are advised to bring forward the review.

These revised forms are intended, together with the Assessment and Action Records, to form a streamlined system for gathering information, planning and review. There remain, however, a number of conceptual difficulties that need to be overcome before they can be properly implemented. Firstly, not all users appreciated that the materials can replace paperwork which is already in use rather than add to it. In a number of instances workers completed the local authority's forms as well as those provided by the project — and complained about the amount of duplication involved. The less workers understood the purpose of the paperwork, the more they regarded it as an unnecessary, bureaucratic imposition, and the more they were likely to complete it unthinkingly, resenting duplication rather than questioning such anomalies.

A similar degree of confusion was apparent over the purpose of planning and review meetings. A number of social workers held the view that the review meeting should be restricted to a simple monitoring exercise, and that additional meetings needed to be arranged if there were a question of altering the plans for a child. This issue has also been raised in research currently being undertaken by the National Children's Bureau (Sinclair and Grimshaw, forthcoming). Apart from the obvious drawback that additional, and possibly overlapping, meetings add to the pressures on limited social work time, this is not how we interpret the Children Act guidance. It is our understanding that the review should be used to examine and assess the care plan and to make appropriate adjustments in the light of subsequent developments. Both the original and the current *Looking After Children* Review Forms are therefore intended as partners to the Care Plans and Placement Plans.

Feedback from users suggests that all the materials can be seen as a bureaucratic exercise and that frequent repetition would be counterproductive. They suggest that, although the Planning and Review forms should be used for all looked after children, the Assessment and Action Records should only be completed for those who are looked after for six months or more. From then onwards, they should be used every six months for children under five and once a year for those aged five or over. (Exact details of how the Records should be tied in with statutory reviews are given in the *Looking After Children Training Guide* and the *Looking After Children Management and Implementation Guide*). From about the age of 17, teenagers begin to find the assessments intrusive and they might be given the opportunity to opt out if the procedure comes to be regarded as counterproductive. Because a high proportion of looked after children quickly return home, a programme such as the above would mean that the Assessment and Action Records would only be used with about a third of children who enter care or accommodation each year. There would, of course, be no reason why, if they considered it appropriate, authorities should not make additional arrangements to assess other children, such as those who are frequently accommodated for brief periods.

If the main benefit of completing the Records is to raise appropriate issues and engender discussion, it seems likely that their usage will diminish over time. When carers and social workers have become thoroughly familiar with their contents they will no longer need the written materials to set an agenda for necessary work with children. If the Records are used as monitoring instruments, with an efficient supervisory system in place to check that plans are properly made and carried out, then they will be used as part of a dynamic procedure for each child, and their value will be less likely to diminish; they will, of course, need to be updated as our knowledge of the key parenting issues increases.

Conclusion

The looked after group was studied over a period of about eighteen months, between October 1991 and June 1993. By the end of this period the evaluation study had been overtaken by events, and the application of the materials to all children looked after by an authority had become a major issue. It will be remembered that there was no expectation that participating authorities might continue to use the materials after the conclusion of the research. However, at the end of the study, two of the four authorities decided to implement the Assessment and Action Records with all their looked after children. The third is still using them with small numbers of selected children within the area which undertook the research. The fourth authority had only a rudimentary monitoring structure in place at the time the research began; it has devoted attention to the construction of a comprehensive review and planning system, developed in consultation with the research team. In every authority it has become apparent that the implementation of the Assessment and Action Records requires the existence of an accepted system for making plans and reviewing children's cases on a regular basis.

Although the findings from the research cannot be applied uncritically to plans to implement *Looking After Children* as part of social work practice across a local authority, they do, nevertheless, identify a number of issues that need to be considered. The most relevant are likely to be those where the findings described in this chapter match the theoretical predictions of Chapter Five. As anticipated, some practitioners have expressed fears that the introduction of explicit practice tools that guide them through the complex responsibilities of the corporate parent might reduce the professional task to 'social work by numbers'. There have also been some concerns about the increase in bureaucracy, and sometimes an almost wilful refusal to regard the materials as more than additional paperwork. Nevertheless, there has been relatively little resistance to the concept of introducing formal assessment procedures to child care services: obstacles are much more likely to arise through failures to appreciate the purpose and value of the exercise for the children concerned, or through inadequate planning or supervision structures than through a lack of interest on the part of practitioners. Both the theoretical predictions and the empirical findings have not only influenced the revisions to the Records but also the national programme for implementation. The in-depth study of implementation in one of the authorities contributing to the research described in the next chapter, demonstrates this more clearly.

At the beginning, we envisaged *Looking After Children* being used by researchers for specific projects within local authorities. As the developmental work got underway, it became clear that implementation across a local authority would be necessary if practitioners and managers were to realise the full potential of the materials. At the end, we were faced with the prospect of 40 local authorities showing a serious interest in various aspects of the project and the distant possibility that *Looking After Children* would eventually be adopted by social services departments across the country. If this is to happen, several obstacles identified in this chapter will need to be overcome.

Summary Points

1. Although practitioners were enthusiastic about completing initial assessments they found it difficult to repeat the process a year later. The problem appeared to be more closely related to the frequency with which the children moved or changed social worker than to a lack of commitment to the research. If implementation is to be successful it will need to be undertaken on an authority-wide basis.

2. Although the Records were usually used successfully as discussion documents, in a number of instances little effort was made to plan improvements on the basis of the information gathered. Supervisors can play an important part in monitoring the construction of plans and identifying inconsistencies.

3. The Records are most likely to be used on a regular basis if they are introduced as an integral part of a structure for planning and review. The Planning and Review forms that accompanied the original Records have been developed and strengthened so that the whole package now forms a streamlined case management system. Revisions were undertaken in close collaboration with policy makers and practitioners with the firm objective of reproducing on paper the informal procedures which parents undertake as a matter of course.

4. There is always a danger that the introduction of high-quality paper-based tools will be resented as an unnecessary bureaucratic imposition. Successful implementation will require adequate training of practitioners and clear policies on when and how the materials should be used. The more practitioners understand their purpose the less they will object to their introduction.

Chapter 7

Implementation in Authority C

Introduction: Profile of the Local Authority

So far we have described some of the potential barriers to implementing *Looking After Children* and have drawn messages from those local authorities which have used the materials during the development phase. This chapter considers in greater depth how implementation proceeded in Authority C. We chose to highlight this authority partly because it has been involved with the project since its inception and, more significantly, because over the past five years it has piloted all the *Looking After Children* materials, using a range of different approaches. At the close of the current stage of the research the authority had begun to use the materials with all its looked after children.

Authority C is a large shire county which includes sizeable pockets of inner-city and rural deprivation alongside affluent commuter-belt country. The authority has a population of 1.5 million, including 355,000 children and young people. Only two per cent of the population are from minority ethnic groups, most commonly from Chinese, New Commonwealth (India, Pakistan and Bangladesh) and Caribbean communities.

Within the authority, social services are delivered from three districts which comprise 17 area centres. The budget is devolved to the districts, with the result that headquarters staff retain an advisory role with few operational responsibilities. There are central support teams, a service quality unit, a

training and personnel unit and a community care implementation team. The significant people are arguably the area
managers (who control the budgets), the service managers
(who prioritise the workloads) and the team managers and
practitioners who deal with clients face to face. The social
workers specialise in work with either children or adults.

Before it began to participate in the research in 1989, the
authority had already adopted policies which were, in many
respects, congruent with the aims and objectives of *Looking
After Children*. Services were based on the principles which
underpin the *Children Act 1989* and for some time the
authority had been giving attention to the quality of parenting
provided by its carers. Partnerships were valued at all levels of
the system and the benefits of making contingency plans rather
than responding reactively to crises were emphasised to
practitioners. The authority had also embraced a further key
principle of the Act, that, wherever possible, services would be
provided to enable children to live at home.

Partly as a result of these policies, the number of children
looked after in the authority has fallen steadily from 2,300 in
1987 to about 1,000 in 1993. The use of foster care has
increased during the same period, while the proportion of
children placed in residential care has remained constant at
16%. Residential care is now primarily being used for teenagers
and more and more children are being placed within the county
boundaries, wherever possible near to home.

All the field social workers in the authority are qualified;
although there is a commitment to train the majority of
residential staff, most are unqualified and a significant
proportion are relatively inexperienced. Partly for this reason,
the authority has invested heavily in family placement
schemes, which include the recruitment of both mainstream
and specialist foster carers. Just over 10% of foster carers have
received specialist training. Increasingly, there has been a trend
for direct work with children to be undertaken by carers, thus
giving them skills appropriate to using the *Looking After
Children* materials; in this authority there was already a

tradition of sharing the social work task between fieldworkers and qualified carers. A training programme which gave equal emphasis to all personnel in the social services departments meant that additional skills could be learned as needed. Fears that *Looking After Children* might be seen as diminishing the professional skills of social workers are likely to have been much reduced in this authority by an acknowledgement that the main users would be the less highly trained carers, who tended to welcome the guidance the materials provided.

When introducing policy developments, the authority encourages representation at all levels of the organisation. The authority has described its commitment to 'the comprehensive development of systems, structures, good policies and practice guidance which will guarantee the involvement of young people in whatever service they receive, regardless of age and ability'. The seriousness with which the authority has taken its commitment to involve users in decision-making processes was illustrated by a series of conferences held in 1993 designed to gather children's perspectives on the services they receive.

Prior to our involvement, the authority had experienced difficulties in constructing planning and review procedures suitable for the 1,000 children looked after each year. As part of the preparations for the implementation of the *Children Act 1989* a basic reviewing system had been developed. Although this identified the key stages, format and procedures for practitioners to follow, the devolved management structure had allowed each area to devise its own separate procedures and the need for a more consistent approach was gradually becoming apparent. The need to introduce a common assessment, planning and reviewing system throughout the county was highlighted by the frequent movements of children in care or accommodation. *Looking After Children* became available just as the county's reviewing policy was being reconsidered.

In ideological and organisational terms, therefore, there were good reasons why the implementation of *Looking After Children* would be successful in this authority; there were, however, a number of practical obstacles to overcome. Before examining the difficulties, it is first useful to consider the benefits the *Looking After Children* system was expected to bring.

Attractions of *Looking After Children* to the Authority

The deputy director of the authority came to the first presentation the researchers made about the project in 1988 and his continuing interest has been fundamental to the subsequent adoption of the materials. The preliminary trials demonstrated that implementation is not possible without the involvement and interest of senior managers and their support has consistently been a key factor in the decision to introduce the *Looking After Children* system in this and other authorities.

As we have seen, the authority was already examining assessment and planning systems. Managers in Authority C were particularly attracted to the potential of the Assessment and Action Records to track patterns and trends of children looked after and produce aggregated data about outcome. The generation of this type of information was seen as a potential means of guiding policy changes and directing resources. The authority was also interested in the possibility of linking the computerised *Looking After Children* materials to its existing information technology systems. It decided to make a cautious investment in the Records in the hope that they would provide consistent information about the quality of services that might lead to a more rational use of resources.

Chapter Five predicted that potential users might be suspicious of the Department of Health's involvement in the development and implementation of the project materials on the grounds that this represented unwarranted interference in local government and, indeed, in the professional judgements of social workers. This is one of the main reasons why the materials have not been made mandatory. However, this was not the experience in Authority C nor in any of the other pilot authorities. Indeed, once it became clear that *Looking After Children* had the backing of central government, managers in the authority appreciated that the experience of their staff could be used to inform and modify the system. Early involvement gave the authority a head start in preparing for implementation, as well as improved insight into central government initiatives. By customising the materials and incorporating them into its own planning and review procedures, the authority retained local control and eased staff suspicions that an alien system was being imposed upon them from above. Indeed, many practitioners felt empowered by the experience of participating in and influencing an initiative that was being promoted nationally.

Testing the Materials in Authority C

Authority C has been involved in the research and development of *Looking After Children* since 1989, when it took part in the preliminary trials. In 1990 it was one of four authorities invited to assess children for the looked after group as part of the current evaluation study. On this occasion it was only able to support the research on a limited basis because of the major restructuring of the social services department prior to the implementation of the *Children Act 1989*. After a quota had been agreed, the authority chose to select for assessment a group of children who had either experienced multiple moves in foster care, or who were living in one of five residential units. Participants were briefed by the research team and, by January 1992, the first assessments were completed. As Chapter Six indicates, more were received than were originally requested.

Formal feedback was given by the research team in September 1992. Completed Assessment and Action Records had identified a number of deficiencies in the service provided to looked after children, including limited availability of schooling in one area, a failure to address the need for therapeutic services for children with severe emotional and behavioural difficulties and inadequate information about the frequency of moves. During this stage the Records were not linked to the statutory reviewing systems and were, to some extent, completed in a vacuum. Staff found it difficult to repeat many of the assessments a year later, as by that time several children had moved on and two of the five residential units had been closed for refurbishment.

Residential social workers and foster carers were given the responsibility for completing the Records. Although this proved to be a highly successful strategy, there were problems. Some residential staff, although prepared by both their managers and the research team, saw the Records as an unnecessary additional task; in one unit staff completed them as a paper exercise, without conferring with the children themselves. Residential staff also had difficulty in organising their work in such a way that they could make the necessary time available for the direct work with a child that the Records require. Carers also sometimes failed to appreciate that the Records could be used to improve care plans and to check that these were carried out. There was also no mechanism for aggregating the information collected, which meant that a key objective, namely to highlight gaps and needs on a coherent basis, could not be met.

The authority responded to these difficulties by incoroporating *Looking After Children* into a revised reviewing structure. It also identified the need for preparation, training and follow-up and an implementation group was formed. An attempt was made to pilot all or part of the system in a secure unit and two area offices.

The experience of piloting the Assessment and Action Records in the secure unit was the least successful. Here, the staff agreed to use the Records with all new admissions over a three month period, thus keeping the boredom factor to a minimum but also generating useful information. However, background details about the many young people coming from outside the authority were often sketchy and the assessment system occasionally clashed with that used by other agencies. In addition, some key workers found the Records excessively long, given that many of the residents were in their care for only a few days. Nevertheless, managers still felt that, in principle, the materials were potentially useful, though probably not for very temporary residents.

One of the two participating area offices chose only to pilot the Planning and Review forms. Problems arose because the local authority forms were still in use and practitioners were unclear as to which system applied when; as one social worker commented, 'We need to have the old forms taken out of the drawers and a list made up to show what we are meant to be using now and what is redundant'. The second area office piloted all the materials and found the experience more rewarding.

Throughout the pilot stages, Authority C continued to identify issues about timing, preparation, usage and training which were passed on to its implementation group. At the end of this period the authority concluded that *Looking After Children* should be promoted in all districts, initially by asking each social worker to identify one child on their caseload with whom to complete an Assessment and Action Record. Gradually staff began to use the materials more flexibly and to share their experiences with colleagues.

The implementation group produced a timetable for introducing the *Looking After Children* system throughout the authority and linking it to other care management procedures and arrangements for meeting inter-agency requirements. Quality assurance measures were also set in place. A training programme was developed and social workers, carers and residential staff were all expected to attend three half-day workshops designed to introduce them to the materials. As this study came to a conclusion, the *Looking After Children* materials were being used for all children looked after or accommodated by the authority.

Authority C implemented the *Looking After Children* materials as they were being developed. During the period of its own implementation programme the authority was also involved in the evaluation and redesign of the Planning and Review forms and the Assessment and Action Records and the development of the *Looking After Children Training Resources Pack*. The development work being undertaken with the research team alongside the authority's programme for implementation meant that, in the early stages, the latter was not methodically planned and, with the benefit of hindsight, some pitfalls could have been avoided. On the other hand, the authority was able to draw on information from the research team and from other authorities taking part in the evaluation study. The rather *ad hoc* implementation process that emerged is likely to prove a useful model for the introduction of new procedures.

General Themes Arising from Authority C's Involvement

Practitioners, staff and carers found that participating in the development and implementation of *Looking After Children* raised a number of issues. The authority has a policy to promote the use of residential care where appropriate and chose to involve its residential units in piloting the Assessment and Action Records. The experiences of residential staff who undertook the assessments identified the need for training before implementation could be successful. Although the questions were largely answered, staff sometimes found it difficult to make time to do the intensive work required with individual children; in some units the need to complete the Records in partnership was not appreciated and young people who had little motivation and inadequate literacy skills were left to respond to the Records on their own. Residential staff also sometimes found it difficult to use the evidence they had collected to plan improvements in practice: for instance, it was noted that, although valuable information about children's health and education had been identified, this had not been used to change the experiences of the young people themselves.

Residential staff were particularly concerned about the potential of the Records to highlight issues of accountability. Key workers' worries that the materials might be used to monitor and criticise their work were given substance by the comments of one manager of a residential unit who welcomed their potential to provide a 'benchmarking tool for staff performance'; he suggested that the Records could be used in supervision sessions to explore issues of accountability. On the other hand, he in his turn was doubtful whether '(senior) managers would be happy to own a system that consistently identifies holes that cannot be filled'. In expressing this opinion, he voiced a concern that the research team repeatedly encountered. A number of senior managers in the authority were indeed worried that the data collected by the Assessment and Action Records on the deficiencies of the service could be used as a source of criticism, if not litigation. One legal adviser regarded this as a reason for not collecting the information at all.

Unlike some residential workers, fieldworkers were not concerned by the complexity of the paperwork and generally welcomed the design. As one put it: 'You don't ask the same question in the same way for every child. Each child is different. This is not a tick box exercise. Each question opens up an area and prompts another 20'. They did, however, consider that the Assessment and Action Records would become counterproductive if they were used so frequently that the task became mechanical; indeed, as we predicted in Chapter Five, some practitioners expressed concerns that the Records might constrain their professional freedom. Practitioners were also conscious that the time needed to complete the Records, about three or four hours spread over several sessions, might not be appreciated by senior management.

Foster carers, especially those working on the specialist scheme, proved to be the strongest advocates for *Looking After Children*, viewing it as acknowledging, validating and making explicit their role. They welcomed the benefits to the children for whom they are responsible, as the following comments demonstrate:

> It gives all the children the same chances. Nothing and nobody gets unnoticed. Lots of different things are drawn to our attention. It can help children's self esteem. It can also remind social workers and people working with these children of their and our responsibilities. However, how the questions are asked and who asks them is critical — knowing the child is essential. These forms really help in working with parents and the school . . . .

Practitioners and carers in Authority C were able to use their experience to make recommendations to the research team about how the Assessment and Action Records should be used and developed. This authority initially decided that the person closest to the child, usually a residential worker or foster carer, was in the best position to co-ordinate the completion of the Records. However, not all were sufficiently trained: the family placement team estimated that only about one in ten foster carers possessed the skill, expertise and motivation to co-ordinate the exercise; almost all of these were project carers or foster carers who had been recruited since the implementation of the *Children Act 1989*. There were also concerns about whether fieldworkers could legitimately hand over this responsibility. Eventually it was decided that the social worker should retain responsibility for co-ordinating the work, even if his or her contribution to the gathering of information was minimal, and most of the face-to-face work with the child and the consultation with relatives and colleagues in health and education should be delegated to residential staff and foster carers. This arrangement is now being followed by most agencies using *Looking After Children*.

Practitioners and carers also played a part in the decision to alter the age-bands for the Assessment and Action Records for older teenagers. They were among several participants who found the Records particularly useful in working with young people who were on the point of leaving care or accommodation. The *Children Act 1989* (S.24.1) and the associated guidance make it clear that 'preparation for leaving care must start well before a young person ceases to be looked after or accommodated and is likely to continue until well after he has done so.' Local authorities are also required to provide after-care for young people who cease to be looked after when aged 16 or over, until they reach 21. This authority is one of a number of agencies which interpret this guidance as requiring them to begin preparing young people for independent living from their fifteenth birthday onwards. That was one reason why social workers in Authority C thought that it would be best for 15-year-olds to use the Record for young people aged 16 and over, which identifies issues which need to be addressed as teenagers move towards independence. The research team has reservations about this interpretation of the guidance, for it appears to encourage the premature placement of 16-year-olds in independent living. Nevertheless, they agreed to alter the age-range for this Record partly because there were other reasons why 15-year-olds should be more appropriately placed in the older grouping and also because they were well aware that, for many young people looked after, independence at 16 is an unfortunate reality.

Practitioners and carers also raised issues about the disclosure of confidential information during the completion of the materials; it is partly due to their concern that the training materials now offer clear guidance, both in relation to child protection disclosures and the more general problems of the sharing of sensitive information. One such question that needed addressing was 'to whom do the Records belong?' The advice was that, technically, the Records remain the property of the social services department, but that the young person should have access to them. The authority intends that young people should receive copies of all *Looking After Children* materials completed during the period that they are looked after. Another pressing question was 'where will the Records be kept?' In order to reduce the risk of the Records being mislaid, it was decided that they should remain in the young person's file but that carers should have ready access to them. Unfortunately, there can be no easy resolution to these administrative difficulties.

Conclusion

Authority C has been involved with this project for six years. Within that time it has implemented several major pieces of legislation and changed from a centralised organisation to one in which both decision-making and budgets are devolved to districts and area teams.

The authority's lengthy involvement with the project inevitably entailed a number of costs. It is important to recognise that implementing *Looking After Children* required the introduction of a completely new planning and review system. Most authorities welcome the opportunity to test experimental procedures, but may be less sure about changes on this scale and with such far-reaching ramifications. Replacing all the authority's planning and review forms with new materials was an expensive investment, despite the concessions that could be made through licensing arrangements. Moreover, staff experienced added pressures through being encouraged to participate in a pilot, or series of pilots, which inevitably competed with other priorities. There were resentments as some staff asked why it was necessary to make changes when the tried and tested system was 'good enough' and in any event skilled staff would be 'doing it all anyway'. Some sceptics remarked that a form remains a form and, however useful, paperwork still represented another stigmatising feature of the care system for young people.

On the other hand, there were considerable benefits. Firstly, as has been seen, social workers, carers and children saw their comments and experiences used to refine materials that were increasingly being introduced on a national basis. Playing a part in the developmental phase of the project enabled participants to retain a sense of ownership of *Looking After Children* and strengthened their commitment to the principles on which it is based. Both this and other participating authorities regarded the opportunity to influence the development of the materials as a major advantage and, as a result, the research team recommend that some part of the system, perhaps the Planning and Review forms, be left open for local adaptations.

Secondly, the introduction of *Looking After Children* promoted a debate about the nature and purpose of planning meetings in relation to the statutory review requirements laid down by the *Children Act 1989*. The formal guidance to the Act states that:

> Reviews form part of a continuous planning process — reviewing decisions to date and planning future work. The purpose of the

review is to ensure that the child's welfare is safeguarded and promoted in the most effective way throughout the period he is looked after or accommodated. Progress in safeguarding and providing for the child's welfare should be examined and monitored at every review and the plan for the child amended as necessary to reflect any significant change (Department of Health, 1991c).

However, the research demonstrated that, within the authority, there was considerable disagreement as to the extent to which reviews could be used as formal planning meetings. *Looking After Children* enabled managers to resolve this question by ensuring that gaps within the child care planning system were identified and addressed.

Thirdly, *Looking After Children* also highlighted potential conflicts between competing child care priorities, such as those between child protection and family support or child welfare and juvenile justice. Practitioners tended to think of children as being placed in one category or another, but the Records showed that many of these overlap, leading to unnecessary duplication of tasks. *Looking After Children* charts a young person's care career and identifies points where such issues need further clarification. *Looking After Children* does not help social workers decide whether or not a child should be looked after but, once that decision has been made, it does show where a range of supports and interventions might be used to meet identified needs.

Finally, as had been hoped, there was evidence that *Looking After Children* reinforced the reciprocal links between quality assurance and management information systems. As a result of this it was easier to direct resources effectively.

By documenting the experiences of Authority C, we have tried to show how the ideas developed by the original working party were tested empirically and have been translated by a process of trial and error into a workable tool to be used in the field. The last three chapters have identified a number of issues that need to be addressed by agencies planning to implement *Looking After Children*. If social services are to get a reasonable return for their investment, they will need to provide the levels of support and support mechanisms evident in this authority. Its experience has confirmed that many of the difficulties predicted do indeed exist, but that they are surmountable. Perhaps the most important point to recognise is that the introduction of *Looking After Children* is likely to be a lengthy business and that managers, practitioners and staff will need to be prepared to recognise and deal with problems as they arise: successful implementation cannot be achieved overnight.

Summary Points

1. The implementation procedure of one large authority that looks after 1,000 children and young people was scrutinised in detail. In this authority the management structure and the budgets are largely devolved to 17 area centres. Each area had its own review procedure, but the need for a more consistent approach had become apparent by the time the *Looking After Children* materials became available. Increasingly this authority uses social workers as co-ordinators, while the direct work with children is largely undertaken by front-line carers.

2. The authority was attracted by the concepts of partnership and corporate parenting which underpin both the philosophy of the project and its own child care policies. It initially decided to take part in the research in the hope that formal assessments would lead to more rational use of resources. The authority was particularly interested in the possibility of aggregating and analysing detailed information about looked after children.

3. Through participating in the research, the authority discovered a need for preparation and training. Several children were not followed up when they moved to new placements away from carers who had originally agreed to participate. Others were left to assess themselves when residential staff failed to appreciate the need to complete assessments in

partnership with children and young people. There were particular difficulties in using the Assessment and Action Records with young people who were temporarily resident in a secure unit.

4. Following the initial research, the authority recognised a need to introduce a comprehensive planning and review system and several pilots of all or parts of *Looking After Children* were set up. These showed that there were serious obstacles to implementing the Planning and Review forms without the Assessment and Action Records. A decision was made to implement the whole system on a gradual basis, steered by a working group.

5. Implementation in this authority has enabled researchers and policy makers to identify how the Assessment and Action Records should be completed and by whom; users have taken a prominent role in developing the materials further and clarifying training issues. Participation in the research project initially has entailed costs in time and resources; however, there have been the benefits of identifying gaps in the child care planning system and reinforcing the link between quality assurance and management systems.

Part Four
Collecting and using the information

Chapter 8

From a practice tool to a data-collecting instrument

Introduction

As we have seen, the Assessment and Action Records serve a number of different purposes. As large-scale implementation has become a pressing issue their value as discussion documents has been increasingly stressed, for it is this aspect that will be most immediately helpful to front-line users: carers, parents, field and residential social workers, and of course the young people concerned. Successful implementation on a regular basis will entail setting the Records within a planning and review system; and this will involve team leaders and reviewing officers. However, their full potential will not have been exploited unless managers, planners and researchers begin to extract quantifiable data from the completed forms, and use these as evidence for directing resources. The Records are only likely to become embedded within the policies and practices of an organisation when their potential has been recognised at all these levels.

Gathering Data

We need, therefore, to ask one final question: can the Records be used as a means of gathering both accurate and useful data about the way in which local authorities are meeting their obligations towards the children for whom they share responsibility? In particular, do they gather reliable, quantifiable data about the outcomes of interventions by social services departments?

The type of information which is of use to managers will not be so extensive as that needed by those who use the Assessment and Action Records as a blueprint of parental tasks. Managers, planners and researchers need information which can be aggregated and analysed to reveal how the available resources can be better deployed in order to meet the needs of looked after children. Concrete information about the quality of care which children receive is important. However, perhaps of greater significance to senior managers are data on patterns of service provision and outcomes. Few authorities at present, for instance, regularly collect and analyse information about the GCSE results of looked after children, or their immunisation records; aggregate information is rarely available about the frequency of offences, the incidence of drug abuse or the rate of teenage pregnancies amongst young people for whom a local authority has accepted long-term responsibilities. Without this routine knowledge, it is difficult for managers to decide how to prioritise demands on the service.

The Assessment and Action Records have the potential to provide such information for those who bear responsibility for the effectiveness of social services. It is largely for this reason that the Records have been used by research teams around the world. However, researchers complete the Records themselves and are usually scrupulous about the accuracy of the information assembled; practitioners and carers have different concerns, and may not give such close attention to detail. We have therefore reconsidered the data from the 204 children in the looked after group to see how far the collection of accurate information was a consideration for practitioners.

Inaccuracies

While researchers are not accountable for outcomes, and therefore have little vested interest in presenting inaccurate data, the issue is by no means so clear for carers and social workers. Most of those who use the Records as practice tools face a conflict of interests: if a child is not being well looked after, should respondents provide accurate information which might lay them open to criticism, or should they try to fudge the issue? In spite of this consideration, we had few indications that respondents lied. Occasionally a carer disputed a social worker's response, or vice versa, but the only obvious instance of deception was where a group of young people had been left to complete the Records by themselves and clearly did not regard this as a serious exercise. There were, however, numerous instances where respondents tended to paint the picture in a more favourable light than was warranted by the evidence. We suspect that this reflected a desire not to denigrate the young people concerned, or in some instances too great a familiarity with disturbed behaviour to appreciate its severity, rather than a deliberate intention to mislead. Further training on the need for objectivity and the recommendation that the Records should be completed by groups of people who can verify each others' contribution will guard against some of these inaccuracies.

The major problem, however, is not deliberate falsification but rather a failure to appreciate the need to provide accurate information. It was relatively common to find instances where the data were quite clearly inaccurate: by the time of the second assessment, for instance, several children appeared not only to have lost weight, but also *height*; others had had *fewer* changes of carer than had been recorded a year previously. In one authority it was possible to check changes of carer as noted by practitioners on the Records against placement changes recorded by administrative staff: the former consistently underestimated the amount of disruption in children's lives.

While inaccuracies can be relatively easily detected with objective data, they are much harder to identify when assessments rest on perceptions. We already know that there can be wide differences between the perceptions of children and those of their carers. Grimshaw (1993) used data from the Assessment and Action Records in an analysis of the emotional and behavioural problems of children attending residential special schools. He found that while there were fairly strong correlations between staff and pupils' reports of visible problems, such as temper tantrums in the classroom, there was little significant agreement over less visible items, such as solvent abuse, nail-biting or disobedience at home. Although the revised Records contain checks which are designed to eradicate bias as far as possible, it is unlikely that it will be removed entirely.

Where the Records required respondents to make deductions, a number of illogicalities were also found. A very large number of children who ate sweets every day were regarded as having a satisfactory diet. Some teenagers who were over the 90th centile nevertheless had their weight assessed as being 'within normal limits for their age'. Several of the children whose behaviour indicated a considerable degree of distress, were regarded as having no particular difficulties; for instance, one 16-year-old boy was sometimes involved in delinquent behaviour 'such as stealing, vandalism or arson'; he fairly regularly displayed abusive behaviour and sleeping problems; he was often defiant and disruptive at school and frequently found it difficult to concentrate. Yet his social worker assessed him as having almost no 'serious emotional or behavioural problems'.

Inaccuracies and illogicalities such as these were relatively common, and some means should therefore be found of reducing them if the Records are to produce reliable data. Some inaccuracies will not necessarily be damaging to children, for when the Records are used as practice tools, the fact that an issue has been brought to the attention of respondents may be more important than the reply that was recorded. It is to be hoped, for instance, that the carer who pretended to attend school parents' evenings and liaise with teachers on a regular basis when, in fact, she had had no contact, would have been encouraged to rectify the omission once the lie had been written down, if only for fear of being found out.

However, other inaccuracies can cause serious difficulties. Social workers who do not know that a child has had several previous placements may underestimate the damage caused by the next move; those who assess obviously disturbed children as showing no significant behavioural difficulties are denying them the opportunity of receiving the help they need. Practitioners are unlikely to gather more accurate data for its own sake, but if they can see how inaccuracies affect the children for whom they are responsible, they might begin to appreciate that greater attention is needed. As Chapter Five has pointed out, the less carers and social workers understand and value the purpose of completing the Assessment and Action Records, the greater will be their resistance to using them; one might add that the less they appreciate the value of collecting data, the less attention they will give to accurate recording.

The Purpose of the Exercise

Nevertheless, even when practitioners appreciate the value of collecting accurate data, they still find it a somewhat alien exercise, for their perceptions of the purpose of gathering information can be very different from those of a researcher. For example, the emotional and behavioural development dimension in the Records asks respondents to rate the frequency with which children display a number of behavioural characteristics. From a research point of view, the purpose of asking these questions is to discover whether children are displaying significant emotional and behavioural problems, and whether they are receiving sufficient help to overcome them. The original questions, therefore, asked respondents to rate the frequency of difficult behaviours; although most children display some of these characteristics at some time or another, if several occur frequently they can be indicative of serious disturbance. The data showed that, although some children in both the looked after group and the community group displayed serious behaviour problems, as suspected, the incidence was much greater among looked after children. They also showed that, while almost three-fifths of the looked after group were thought to have serious problems, only a very small proportion (16%) were currently receiving professional help.

From a manager's view these data are obviously valuable, as they can be used to identify where expensive resources should best be directed. In the revised Records the original questions have been replaced with indicators of disturbance taken from validated instruments and a research project is now testing how far responses will facilitate the early identification of children who need specialist help. If assessments of behaviour patterns are undertaken on a regular basis, it should be possible to map changes and identify the extent to which improvements are linked to particular interventions.

Yet, though managers and researchers regard the collection of such information as a valuable advance, social workers and carers, who will be responsible for recording it, are more sceptical. Although the identification of problematic behaviour patterns is the key issue for managers, practitioners object that such a focus can reinforce the poor image of looked after children and convey the message that bad behaviour is to be expected. The revised Records try to to mitigate this effect by introducing indicators of positive behaviour, but this will not solve the underlying mismatch between different perceptions.

Social workers and carers value the opportunities that the Records provide for opening up discussions with looked after children and strengthening relationships, and we assume that this has benefits for the children themselves. They tend, however, to overlook the purpose of the assessment, which should not be simply to describe how children are progressing, but to analyse how they might be further helped. The role of the social worker, in particular, is to be more than the child's best friend: dispassionate and objective identification of how children might be helped to achieve better behavioural outcomes should be regarded not as a de-personalising procedure, but as an integral part of the professional task. This is a major training issue for it involves a shift in attitudes, from seeing assessment largely as a means of describing and

152

exploring a child's behaviour, to regarding it as an analytic procedure which can lead to improvements in practice.

Assessments of Objectives

Practitioners may further appreciate the need for dispassionate analysis when they understand the uses to which it can be put. The assessment of objectives at the end of each dimension of the Records is intended to provide an indication of the child's progress towards those objectives which hold the key to successful development. However, if accurate data are properly collected and aggregated, they can show how outcomes for an individual child alter over time, as Chapter Nine illustrates.

Although this information can obviously be used to examine how individual children are progressing and identify areas where intensive work needs to be undertaken, it can also be aggregated to demonstrate trends in outcomes for particular groups. There are some indications that group outcomes for the looked after children in the study may have improved by the time of the second assessment: for example, a year after the first assessment the number of children who were judged to be receiving insufficient preventive health care had been reduced; there were fewer children whose educational attainments were considered well below average, and there were more who were acquiring at least some special skills and interests. There was, however, no appreciable difference in the proportion of children whose weight was outside normal limits or the number who smoked regularly.

The Records have been redesigned to try to overcome the original, practical difficulties, but it still remains to be seen whether the assessments of objectives will now be properly completed. Further work is also needed in order to identify ways in which the reliability of the responses can be improved. However, although researchers can refine the capacity of the materials to produce accurate and quantifiable data, we cannot do more than this. Managers and planners who have an interest in collecting these data need to ensure that staff are aware of their purpose and are properly supervised in undertaking the task. The more information that can be fed back to demonstrate how objective evidence about outcomes can be used to benefit individual children, the more readily will practitioners produce it.

Decisions to Take No Further Action

Earlier chapters have demonstrated how the Records quite successfully require respondents to make plans for remedial action when they discover that an essential parental task is not being undertaken, particularly if the assessments are used as part of a comprehensive system for making plans and reviewing children's cases. They are not so successful in obtaining explanations in those instances where omissions have been identified and no such plans have been made.

There will, of course, be certain children for whom the recommended actions are either inappropriate or impossible; although local authorities may welcome the Assessment and Action Records as a blueprint for what might be expected of them in their role as parents, they also need to be able to set priorities within that context. Ordinary parents follow a similar procedure: they tend to have an overall view of what, in principle, their children need, and then to tailor their plans to meet each child's requirements and their own circumstances. For instance, they may initially expect to have their children immunised in order to protect them from disease, but waive this for one child if there are medical contra-indications; they may want their children to have the opportunity to travel, but decide that other, competing demands on the family purse should take priority over a particular school trip. Managers need to have information about how this type of decision is made for looked after children in order to monitor how standards are applied. Yet, by and large, these were the questions that respondents most frequently ignored. For instance, we found that 14 of the 10–15 year olds in the looked after group were not receiving help with school work at home; plans were made to provide assistance for only four, and in just three of the remaining cases was an explanation given as to why this would not be offered.

It is probable that many respondents ignored the request to explain why recommended actions were not being undertaken because they did not understand it, and certainly the number of irrelevant remarks that were offered as replies would lend weight to this view. However, discussions with social workers suggest that there might have been other, more problematic, factors which prevented them from providing this information. Although the researchers repeatedly pointed out that there were good reasons why generally recommended actions would not always be appropriate for specific children, justifications could often read like excuses. Table 8.1 shows the range and type of reasons given for decisions to take no further action on issues raised by the Records; while the fact that a child was not yet old enough could well be a valid reason for inaction, the loss of records, or the failure to allocate a case might appear to offer grounds for further inquiry.

Table 8.1: *Reasons Given for Decisions to Take No Further Action*

Reason for decision	Type of Decision
The child is not old enough	
The child/carer does not want to	Professional
This is not appropriate for this particular child because. . .	
We are waiting for a change of circumstance (eg change of placement) before we can take action	
The records have been lost	
The case has not been allocated	Managerial
We do not have enough money/resources/any provision for this in this area	
This is the responsibility of another agency	

As the previous chapter demonstrates, many managers fear the collection of quantifiable information in case it highlights deficiencies in the service and renders authorities liable to allegations that they are failing in their duties, especially if reasons why there are no accompanying remedial plans are made explicit. Some social workers have similar fears that, as the messengers who bring the bad news, they could be the first in the line of criticism. As one of them pointed out to the researchers:

> of course we know that there are all sorts of things we should be doing for our children that we have neither the time nor the resources to accomplish, but there is no point in writing this all down, as it won't change anything. All we would succeed in doing would be producing yet another stick with which we can be beaten.

And yet, when social workers can be persuaded to provide reasons for inaction, their answers provide just the sort of data that planners need. As the previous table shows, their explanations fall mainly into two distinct categories: those based on factors within the organisation, and those based on professional judgements. Quantifiable information from social workers can be helpful in demonstrating how organisational factors affect the quality of children's experiences. If one four-year-old in foster care cannot attend a playgroup because there is no money to pay the fees, this will not carry much weight, but if 20 four-year-olds have the same experience, then the evidence should be used as grounds for a management decision as to where pre-school education should come in the order of priorities.

The possibility of introducing further checklists to facilitate the collection of these data was considered, but ultimately rejected on the grounds that they would be counterproductive. There is considerable tension between the needs of statisticians and the culture in which social workers operate; although precise and accurate data can best be collected in a standardised manner, there is a view that this type of rigidity will diminish the image of the social worker as a professional. In revising the Assessment and Action Records, wherever possible, questions about social work decision-making have been left open-ended: although the introduction of further checklists might have made it easier to quantify the data, the feedback from respondents suggests that this approach would have been more likely to produce the negative effect of reducing the Records to a form-filling exercise to be completed as fast as possible, in which case the potential benefits of using the materials as discussion documents would have been largely negated.

Matching Needs

The difficulty of aligning materials to meet the requirements of both practitioners and managers is not simply engendered by a clash of cultures. When we came to revise and develop the Basic Facts Sheet (now the Essential Information Record) it was brought sharply home to us that there was only a certain amount of congruence between the needs of those who would use the information it gathered.

The Essential Information Record was originally produced in order to obviate the need for social workers to record the same factual information about a child each time they completed an Assessment and Action Record. The original working party argued that, while the Records could be used to prompt social workers to check that factual information about a child is being recorded, the information itself should be gathered together in one place, and kept where it could be easily accessed on the file (Parker *et al*, 1991). The original Essential Information Record was similar to the information-gathering sheets used by most social services departments, the difference being that it aligned with the Assessment and Action Records.

We know from a number of sources how easy it is for a child to to lose his or her history if looked after for any length of time (O'Neill, 1981; MacVeigh, 1982). Frequent moves can mean that not only names and addresses of relatives, but also information about childhood illnesses or school performance can be lost if they are not written down. The revised Essential

Information Record provides both a historical record of placements and schools attended and also collects current information about, for instance, medication and contact addresses. From the practitioner's point of view, its purpose is both to preserve the details about a child's history and to provide carers with the type of parental knowledge they need to do their job properly. However, managers regard this record as a rich source of information that can be aggregated and used for planning services. That there are tensions between the two views can be seen in the reluctance of some practitioners to record information about children's racial/ethnic background: although on the one hand this is seen as discriminatory, on the other it is seen as necessary for planning the recruitment of foster carers.

The Essential Information Record is now being used in over 40 local authorities. The adoption of a standardised format for gathering information about all looked after children, and perhaps eventually about all children in need, could bring immediate benefits when children move from one authority to another — gains which may be readily apparent at a managerial level if the larger organisations are eventually broken down into smaller authorities. However, again, the potential advantage may not be met with universal enthusiasm: there have been concerns that standardising the way in which this information is gathered will make it more accessible in future litigation.

Although computerisation of the Essential Information Record now facilitates the aggregation of data, it also emphasises the difference in perspective between the various parties concerned. The computer programme will not only analyse information that is of value within each authority, it will also facilitate the collection and aggregation of data at a national level, for it contains an automatic facility to compile the SSDA 903 returns on children looked after required annually by the Department of Health. The paper-based Essential Information Record has also been redesigned to meet this requirement. Just as the information requirements of planners are not entirely congruent with those of individual children, so the needs of central government do not always match those of local authorities. Nevertheless, there is sufficient commonality of purpose for it to make sense to organise the data collected on one document in such a way that it can be used at all three levels.

At present, many social workers are unaware of the requirement to provide annual returns to central government or the insights into practice of the data produced. At a local level, for instance, information about the ages or languages spoken by looked after children can help local authorities to direct resources that meet their needs; at a national level, information about the provision of short-term accommodation for children in need or the frequency of emergency protection orders may indicate where resources are being inappropriately used and provide a basis for inspections. Accurate information is needed for planning purposes, and that can only be gathered from the children to whom it refers. If authorities begin to collect their information in the same way, the pool of data gathered nationally will become more reliable. It should, eventually, be possible to engage in closer discussions at all levels about which information should be collected and aggregated, and for what purposes; if social workers can appreciate how the children for whom they share responsibilities might benefit by the aggregation of data, they are less likely to view the procedure as an unnecessary bureaucratic exercise.

Conclusion

Among all professional groups, social workers seem to find it hardest to accept that the gathering of quantifiable data can serve more than a bureaucratic purpose. Not only may they perceive it as detrimental to their relationship with clients, but also as belittling, for the collection of such information is sometimes seen as depersonalising the individual who provides it. Yet it may be just because this procedure is so often seen as alien that social workers find it difficult to produce evidence of the effectiveness of their interventions.

It is difficult to tell how far the anomalies and inaccuracies discovered in the assessments from our study group have distorted the dataset. Certainly we would advocate the conduct of further tests of accuracy in order to identify ways of improving the quality of responses. We would also emphasise the need for further training and supervision of those who are responsible for completing the Records. It is important for those who administer *Looking After Children* to be aware that not all the data required have to be collected by social workers themselves: it has already been noted that the Records are usually best completed by carers who are most likely to know children well enough to ask personal questions with impunity. Some of the other data, particularly those on the Essential Information Record, can be assembled by administrative staff.

Sharing the workload may make it easier to ensure that the information is gathered, but it is only when the data are fed back in a format that can demonstrably be used to help the children concerned that practitioners are likely to perceive their worth, and recognise the importance of accuracy. The following chapter demonstrates the type of information it is possible to feed back from completed Assessment and Action Records. Although the dataset is in some parts patchy and in others unreliable, it nevertheless provides demonstrably more — and more useful — information about the experiences and progress of looked after children than has previously been available.

Summary Points

1.   If the Assessment and Action Records are to be fully accepted into the culture of an organisation they need to be used as data-collecting instruments as well as discussion documents and planning tools.

2.   While practitioners will need to ensure that all the issues of importance to parents are covered when children are looked after away from home, managers will be interested in much more selective information. However, accuracy will be a more prominent

consideration to those who want information that can be aggregated and analysed as a basis for further planning.

3.   Practitioners are unlikely to gather accurate data unless they appreciate its purpose. Although some inaccuracies will not damage individual children, others will frustrate plans to improve the quality of the care they receive. Studies are needed to discover how responses based on perceptions rather than verifiable evidence can be made more reliable.

4.   Although the revised materials have been designed to gather more accurate data, managers and supervisors will need to take responsibility for ensuring that the Assessment and Action Records are properly completed. Practitioners will need assurance that unwelcome information, such as the ways in which restricted resources affect the quality of care the authority can provide, will be used to benefit the children concerned, and not to criticise their efforts.

5.   Both the computerised and the paper-based versions of the Essential Information Record have been designed to allow for the extraction of data required in annual returns submitted to central government. Practitioners may resent this, and view the accurate completion of other *Looking After Children* materials as a bureaucratic exercise unless they appreciate how aggregated data can be used to improve opportunities for individual children. Frequent feedback on the uses made of the data will therefore be necessary.

Chapter 9

Using information over time

Introduction

In the previous chapter we discussed the potential of the materials to provide local authorities with information that can help improve services for looked after children. As part of the evaluation study we assessed this potential by considering the way in which practitioners completed and used the materials on the 204 children described in Chapter Two. The information produced gives further insight into the experiences of children in care or accommodation and again demonstrates the possible uses of data collected in this way.

It will be recalled that the 204 looked after children were selected to test the Records. Although they comprised a cross-section of children likely to experience care or accommodation, as would be expected by virtue of the task, long-stay cases tended to dominate the group. At the time of the first assessment the majority (62%) were aged ten years or more, one in five lived in residential units and 25% had been looked after for six years or more, with another 60% in care or accommodation for between one and five years. While such a study group is not a random sample and so firm conclusions cannot be drawn, some of the information obtained is relevant to understanding the needs of all looked after children. The breadth of these data and their potential uses are also apparent and can be illustrated by considering some findings in the seven developmental dimensions that make up the Assessment and Action Records.

Health

One area that is greatly illuminated by using the Assessment and Action Records is the child's health. Research has suggested that people who are under emotional stress are particularly vulnerable to illness. For instance, Cohen *et al* (1991) found, in a prospective study, that adults experiencing the effects of negative life events had an increased susceptibility to infection. Some children and young people, especially those who have been looked after from a very early age might, therefore, be regarded as being at high risk of developing emotional difficulties and physical health problems. Bamford and Wolkind (1988) concluded from their review of research on the physical and psychological health of looked after children that 'those who had been in care were gravely disadvantaged as a group [and that] medical examinations of children on admission and during foster home placements are undervalued and often overlooked'. Sir William Utting (Department of Health, 1991b), Chief Inspector of the Social Services Inspectorate, stated that though there were instances where the provision of health care was considered adequate [in residential care], there was evidence that the process of health assessment generally was haphazard and the use of medical services was largely in response to illness. Despite routine medical examinations there was little concern with prevention and health education.

It would therefore be helpful for local authorities to trace the health problems and health care of looked after children on both an individual and an aggregate basis. The Assessment and Action Records gather readily available information about issues such as diet, growth, immunisations, developmental checks, statutory medical examinations and chronic or acute health problems and their treatment. Questions in the older age-ranges gather additional information about health education; they ask not only whether young people engage in behaviours that put their health at risk, but also whether they have been given information about the potential consequences of doing so.

The information assembled on the looked after group confirmed children's vulnerability to illness of sufficient severity to necessitate time off school, most commonly colds, 'flu, or migraine. Although this was probably no surprise, several children had also suffered from combinations of infections, such as might be consonant with a generally poor state of health. For instance, one 10-year-old boy, long in local authority care, had 'a heavy cold, worms, headaches, tonsillitis, urine infection and an ear infection' in the six months prior to assessment. The extent of his condition had not been realised until the social worker completed the Record and she subsequently arranged a medical, which turned out to be long overdue. Similarly, amid a plethora of data on routine hospital appointments, there emerged three girls between the ages of 15 and 17 whose attendance at hospital for treatment for self-inflicted injuries suggested that they were at considerable risk; one had been to hospital on several other occasions suffering from the effects of solvent abuse.

Information gathered during the preliminary trials also demonstrated that health education can be overlooked when children's care is shared by a number of people: for instance, a quarter of the 16-year-olds assessed had received no information about sexually transmitted diseases or contraception. It appeared that neither parents nor carers had regarded sex education as their responsibility, often assuming that this would be undertaken by teachers, and ignoring the possibility that many of the young people had not been in school when this subject was being taught. At the time of the study, this finding caused a flurry of activity, and in the three months between assessments, every young person taking part in the trial was given a crash course in sex education (Ward *et al*, 1991).

The sequential application of the Records helps authorities to see if things have changed or if improvements in practice have been sustained. For example, responses from children in the evaluation study, selected about two years after those in the preliminary trials, showed that 95% of children and young people over the age of ten had received information about the harmful effects of smoking, alcohol, drugs and glue-sniffing and all those aged sixteen or over had received information about sex, contraception and sexually transmitted diseases. While it must, again, be emphasised that this is not based on a random sample, the high figures are encouraging. However, as any parent knows, education about possible consequences is not sufficient to stop young people from taking risks. The Records gather data about behaviour as well as education: only eight of the 14 older teenagers who said they were sexually active always used contraceptives and there had been three pregnancies.

Other health risks were evident. Nearly half (45%) of children over the age of ten said that they smoked regularly and nearly a third (31%) said they drank alcohol. Excessive consumption was a frequent problem for ten youngsters, six of whom also abused other noxious substances such as glue and drugs. The Records highlight health risks that might otherwise go unnoticed and act as a check on other information gathered on children — three of the young people who were thought to over-indulge in alcohol had previously denied that they drank at all.

It is also possible to identify particular care settings where risks are high. For example, a markedly higher proportion of young people looked after who smoked or drank were living in residential units, a finding that is only partly explained by their age. The research team were originally advised that it was pointless to ask whether young people in residential care smoked, as the practice was universal, but, again, this assumption is belied by the more complicated picture revealed by using the Records. Since these data were collected, the Department of Health has issued guidance on smoking and alcohol consumption in such establishments (Department of Health, 1994b); the Records could be used to discover whether such guidance is implemented effectively.

Education

There is now a long catalogue of research on the failure of children looked after to get a satisfactory education (Triseliotis and Russell, 1984; Berridge and Cleaver, 1987; Fletcher-

Campbell and Hall, 1990; Garnett, 1994; Colton, Jackson and Heath, 1994; Jackson, 1994). However, few authorities gather the type of data that would enable them to identify where improvements can be made. They first need straightforward information about educational progress, examination results, further education and the employment of school leavers; this then needs to be related to the type of experiences that looked after children receive while in school: important issues are, for instance, school exclusions, truancy and changes of school. *The Looking After Children Management and Implementation Guide* explains how such information can be extracted and aggregated from the responses to the Records. There is some evidence that authorities are already using the materials for this purpose (see Stephenson and Behan, 1993).

An area to which authorities might give particular attention is the extent to which children in care or accommodation are helped to plan their education and subsequent employment. The data suggest that many children in the looked after group were preoccupied with concerns about relationships with their families and their current situation at a time when their peers were devoting their energy to considering their educational and employment prospects. Evidence from other studies suggests that authorities find it difficult to give adequate and timely attention to educational issues that can have far-reaching effects: for instance, they do not always appreciate the detrimental effects to children of moving school halfway through examination courses, or, as Garnett (1994) found, of residential units closing down just before teenagers are due to sit GCSE examinations. Aggregated data from the Records can demonstrate how children are affected by such decisions and whether long-term educational plans are being made and carried out.

Identity

The Records can also be used to monitor the strengths and weaknesses of carers and to identify further training needs. For instance, many children in the looked after group were considered to lack self-confidence and to suffer from poor self-esteem. Although unconditional regard and approval are generally seen as fundamental to self-esteem, one in five (19%) of the study group seldom or never received loving approval from their carers, many because 'their behaviour was too bad to merit it'. Responses such as these indicate that primary carers may need to be alerted to the need to provide opportunities that enable children to enhance their perceptions of themselves.

The need for life story work is another training issue that might be highlighted through analysis of the data. The Records include guidance on the importance of preserving that information about a child's past which is necessary to the development of a sense of identity. Discussions about the past not only help children to make sense of the disruptions and fragmentary memories they may have of their early lives, but also provide a means of talking about difficult issues. Falhberg (1988) suggests that the process of compiling a life story book can aid children's acceptance of the past and facilitate the development of self-esteem as well as helping them to gain a sense of trust in the person with whom the work is undertaken. Unfortunately this potentially valuable, but time-consuming, work was being undertaken with less than half (45%) of the children who had been looked after for two years or more.

Family and Social Relationships

There is now considerable research evidence which shows that contacts with family members provide most children with a sense of belonging and continuity which it is difficult for local authorities to recreate. Regular contact between looked after children and their natural families can have a positive effect on their well-being while they are living away from home. Almost all looked after children eventually go home, and this process will be smoother if the links between them and their families have been maintained (Triseliotis, 1980; Department of Health, 1991d; Bullock *et al*, 1993). Certainly, the *Children Act 1989*, and more especially the accompanying regulations and guidance, emphasise the importance of sustaining relationships between looked after children and their natural families, and of including birth parents and other relatives in the care process.

The Assessment and Action Records can help local authorities monitor the maintenance of contact between children and their families and identify those whose links are diminishing, in order to take appropriate action. The data gathered from the looked after study group suggested that this continues to be a difficult area and that good quality and up to date information is essential for good practice as situations can change quickly. For instance, for nearly half the children (46%), more needed to be done to promote links with family members while for 13% contact was problematic because parents did not measure up to expectations. Contact was considered by professionals to be detrimental to the child's well-being in just over a quarter of the cases studied. Moreover, about a third of young people were unhappy with access arrangements, and almost all of these said they wanted more, rather than less, contact.

The difficulties faced by young people in care or accommodation who try to live independently are well documented (e.g. Stein and Carey, 1986; Stein, 1990; Bonnerjea, 1990; Biehal *et al*, 1992). Under the *Children Act 1989*, local authorities have a duty to prepare young people for the time when they cease to be looked after and to provide after-care. Three quarters of those aged over 15 who were studied had a home where they could drop in without invitation, expect to go for holidays, be sure of a bed if necessary, and expect help at times of crisis. Almost all of those who were planning to try to live independently when they left the care of the local authority said that this type of support was available to them. The one exception was a girl who, ominously, had nowhere to go for Christmas. However, some of these young people expected the residential unit in which they had been living to provide a safe haven after they had left; responses such as these might need monitoring, as we know that such placements find it difficult to give support for any length of time (Stein and Carey, 1986).

One of the areas where the data suggested that children in the community group might be at some disadvantage compared with children and young people who are looked after was the opportunity to see friends outside school. However, the use of the *Looking After Children* materials, with their focus on the whole child, puts this research finding in its broader perspective. The Records showed that, although most looked after children were said to have some close friends, the majority of these friends were also in care or accommodation. Although immensely strong and supportive relationships can be formed in the face of shared adversity, vulnerable children and young people also need opportunities to interact with peers from a range of circumstances. Children whose main source of friendship is with others who share the low expectations, poor self-esteem and low achievements that characterise so many of those who are looked after tend to become marginalised and alienated from mainstream society and derive their social identity, values and mores from an increasingly narrow group (see also Quinton *et al*, 1993).

Social Presentation

The questions relating to the appearance and care of very young children, of whom there were 24 under the age of two years in the looked after study group, focus on whether babies are bathed and changed when needed as well as on whether they are dressed appropriately for their age. As one would hope, the results showed that all children of this age in the care of a local authority had these basic needs met. Most older children and young people were also suitably dressed, although the clothes of 2% of those over the age of four were not thought appropriate to their age, race or culture. The data did, however, suggest that there was also a small group of seven children whose general appearance gave the impression that they were not well cared for.

It is again possible to use information such as this to monitor the quality of care provided in different settings. For instance, the finding that several children living in a particular residential unit were dirty or wore unwashed, ill-fitting clothes, should be regarded as a reason for action. Elsewhere, responses to questions on identity, social presentation and family and social relationships can be used to identify children who are showing early signs of ostracism and isolation. One 11-year-old said she had no friends, either within or outside the care system; there was no contact at all with her relations, apart from irregular and infrequent visits from a grandmother, yet she had no knowledge of why she was not living with her family. She had had at least eight care placements in the seven years since admission, as well as an unspecified number of school changes that had culminated in her accommodation in a residential unit with an on-site school. Her replies demonstrated very low self-esteem on a number of indicators. Her poor personal hygiene and ill-fitting clothing would have given an impression of someone who was not properly cared for and probably added to her isolation from her contemporaries. The Assessment and Action Records can identify children who show multiple disadvantages such as these, hopefully in time for the local authority to intervene.

Emotional and Behavioural Development

Information from the looked after study group suggested that social workers tended to underestimate the severity of disturbance in some children; they also assumed that extremely challenging behaviour could be handled informally by carers, and only rarely needed to be referred to specialists. In response to this, the Records have been revised to obtain precise information about the ways in which behavioural problems are being managed and to give details of current and past specialist treatment for all emotional and behavioural disorders. Matching a profile of behavioural characteristics against current management should enable supervisors to check that appropriate action is being taken for individual children.

However, identifying those children who need specialist help is not easy and further research into the benefits of using the

Looking After Children materials in this area is needed. The use of the materials raises a number of questions. For instance, is psychological disturbance reflected by the number of behavioural difficulties children exhibit? Can it be argued that a child with one very difficult behaviour may be exhibiting as much disturbance as the child with many which are less severe? Does the severity of the behaviour indicate the level of distress? By severity, do we mean the frequency of occurrence or its seriousness?

A further consideration should be whether the behaviour in question is appropriate for the age and stage of development of the child. For instance, it is common for children under the age of five to wet themselves occasionally, particularly if they are engrossed in what they are doing. However, if a 15-year-old regularly wets the bed, this would suggest emotional distress. There is a the tendency for children to regress following stressful events (Erikson, 1950), and some problematic behaviours might be expected to occur following admission to local authority care or accommodation; these would not in themselves indicate serious emotional or behavioural difficulties unless they showed no signs of settling down within a reasonable time.

Combinations of behaviours may also indicate the severity of the child's disturbance, as the profile of Megan, one of the children studied, illustrates:

> Megan was eight and living in a foster placement when she was assessed. She had no chronic illnesses but had an unspecified physical condition which required regular hospital attendance. There was no indication of how long she had been in the care of the local authority but a number of emotional and behavioural difficulties were evident. These indicated some regression to behaviour one might expect of a much younger child. She could be aggressive, irritable and have tantrums. The foster carer said that Megan's behaviour was not always acceptable to others, that she was often over-excited when in other people's houses and could be 'very noisy and loud.' She frequently told lies or made up fantasy stories. She was often clinging and fearful and sometimes showed no interest in play. She soiled herself

sometimes and could be extremely quiet and shy. On the other hand, she often displayed sexual behaviour and knowledge that were considered inappropriate for her age.

Research and practice issues of this type should be better informed once *Looking After Children* is widely implemented and national data on looked after children become available. Alterations made to the revised version of the Records have been designed to enable them to be used to identify those children who might benefit by specialist referral.

Self Care Skills

The Assessment and Action Records ask respondents to complete a checklist of age-related items about children's self care skills. For instance, the carers of three and four-year-olds are asked whether children are able to take themselves to the toilet and wash their hands; whether they can blow their noses, dress and feed themselves and help tidy away their playthings. In isolation, such detail may seem trivial, but as part of the wider concern about standards of care, its significance can be considerable.

There may be little value in an authority regularly aggregating data on all the everyday issues covered by this dimension, but there are occasions when an analysis can be usefully undertaken for the purpose of training. For instance, the information from the looked after study group suggested that children and young people who lived in residential care generally had fewer self care skills than those in foster homes, a finding useful to a discussion of standards of parenting in different settings. A scrutiny of the self care skills displayed by children looked after in a particular residential unit might also enable staff to identify tasks which could be undertaken to help improve their competence. Such monitoring exercises are, of course, particularly important for seeing how well young people are being prepared to move towards independence.

The Uses of Aggregated Data from a Single Assessment

The discussion so far has identified how the data on individual children can be aggregated by local authorities to provide information that can serve to direct policy and allocate resources. Those who use the data in this way will be able to identify and address the weaknesses in the services provided; the above discussion has focused on some of the difficulties experienced by looked after children which could form the basis for such an exercise.

However, the data should be looked at differently if they are to be used to build up profiles of individual children. It is artificial to separate children's lives into different dimensions, for factors that affect one aspect of their day-to-day experiences will necessarily have ramifications in other areas. Children who are worried about what may be happening at home will probably have difficulty concentrating on their work in school. Conversely, those who find positive reinforcement at school or in other situations, may develop a certain resilience and be much more able to cope with disruptive influences in other areas. Since there are many influences on children's lives, the identification of one influential factor does not illuminate the whole situation. Over-simplification may create feelings of helplessness in carers and policy makers alike and lead to self-fulfilling prophecies.

While managers may need to focus on problems in order to improve the service, it should be noted that the data from the study group showed many instances of children benefiting from high standards of care when looked after away from home. We should be encouraged that many of them seemed to tackle life's tasks with ability and resilience and to deal successfully with the increasing demands made by the transitions into adulthood. Shaun provides a good example:

> Shaun was two and a half when he was first looked after and eight at the time of his first assessment. He had had two placements and two changes of school since admission. For the previous 11 months he had been living with foster carers with

whom he got on very well. They were open with him and had explained why he was being looked after and not living with his family; they gave him positive feedback and the physical affection he needed, though continuity and attachment were regarded as fairly tenuous. He had irregular and infrequent contact with his mother and siblings and saw his grandparents once a year. Nevertheless, he was intelligent, doing well in school and confident in his own abilities. In addition, he belonged to various sports clubs, went to church and had many friends. Despite his past experience of physical and emotional abuse, he was demonstrating no emotional or behavioural problems, could communicate with others and could adjust his behaviour to different situations.

Monitoring Change Over Time

Until now the focus of this chapter has been upon a single application of the Records and the type of information this produces. However, this static view is somewhat artificial for, as Herbert (1993) argues:

> several longitudinal prospective studies have demonstrated that many individuals retain a great capacity for change; the outcomes of the events of early childhood are continually transformed by later experiences, making the course of human development more open than many theorists in the past ever believed possible.

As Chapter Six has reiterated, outcomes cannot be considered in isolation: they are part of a dynamic process in which the ending of one stage becomes the beginning of the next. Moreover, assessments of outcomes need to be linked to children's development; it is rarely possible to hold things steady in one area while issues are addressed in others. It was always intended that the Assessment and Action Records would be used on a regular basis so that progress made by individual children in each of the dimensions could be charted.

When the Assessment and Action Records are used for the same children at regular intervals useful data emerge. Firstly, it is possible to chart the progress made by individual children in each of the seven developmental dimensions. The data can show whether a child is healthier, more confident, better integrated socially and so on, since the last assessment. The materials are useful in this respect since changes affecting children are varied and not all one way. It also seems likely that some improvements are more easily effected than others. Small changes, such as renewing contact with a relative or teaching a young person to use a washing machine are easy to achieve and can be significant in enhancing their quality of life.

A second type of data is produced when aggregated statistics are compared over time. These demonstrate the changing quality of services and identify whether plans for improvement have been effectively pursued. It was established in Chapter Four that if they are to cope effectively, children need to know what is happening to them and why. At the second repetition, Records on the 83 children who were assessed twice showed a 5% reduction in those who were unable to explain why they were not living in their natural families. Furthermore, there was a 16% rise in those undertaking life story work. Social workers' assessments of children's progress concluding the section on identity reflected these improvements as fewer children were regarded as having little understanding of their situation.

Improvements were echoed in the family links of looked after children. It was found that at the first assessment 45% of social workers had felt that more needed to be done to promote contact with natural families. By the second assessment this figure had fallen to 35%, which suggested that efforts had been made to strengthen these links. Indeed, there was a noticeable increase in contact with fathers, grandparents and other family members. Naturally, such evidence needs much closer scrutiny before it can be concluded that improvements have occurred. Nevertheless, data of this kind are easily forthcoming as the Record accumulates.

Combining Individual and Aggregated Data

It is also possible, by combining individual and aggregated data, to explore the relationship between changes in individuals and the altered characteristics of the group. The data pertaining to children's appearance and the acceptability of their conduct in public revealed improvements in both individuals and the overall situation. At the initial assessment a small number of children were identified who had not learnt how to behave in public and who appeared poorly cared for. However, by the second assessment, all of these children had been taught appropriate behaviour and their appearance had changed for the better. The improvement for these individuals was reflected in the aggregated outcome measures which indicated that the proportion of children whose behaviour and appearance were acceptable to others rose between assessments.

But combining different types of data is fraught with difficulty, as inappropriate uses of information produced by the *Looking After Children* materials can illustrate. Firstly, it is necessary to be sure that like is compared with like. Aggregated statistics may show no change in the proportions of children displaying certain features twelve months apart, but it is important to know whether these figures refer to the same children on each occasion. An example concerned current school exclusions, the level of which remained virtually the same (9% and 11%) at the two assessments. When individual children were scrutinised, however, it was found that the eight excluded in the second assessment were different children from those excluded at the first. Children's individual profiles revealed much higher rates of school exclusion, nearly a quarter experiencing rejection at some point during the year; one might assume a higher rate still in the course of an educational career.

Secondly, comparisons between aggregated figures from different agencies or areas within a local authority must be treated cautiously. It is fallacious to infer characteristics about individuals from data about the groups of which they are a part. For instance, if a local authority has a high proportion of looked after children in residential care and high aggregated figures for children absent from school, it cannot be deduced that it is the children in community homes who are not attending. The details of individual cases have to be checked before any conclusions can be reached.

Thirdly, results may also reflect the way in which questions are asked in the Assessment and Action Records or the ages of the children on whom they are completed. This was clear in the questions about health, particularly those that checked immunisations and medical examinations. At the first completion, the Records showed that a high proportion of young people over the age of 10 (64%) had not had a BCG immunisation; though this had improved a year later, 48% were still unprotected. But these findings have to be interpreted in context. BCG immunisations are given when children are aged between 10 and 14 and differences in aggregate statistics may be explained by the increasing age of those studied. On the other hand, local policies might be important as some health authorities restrict immunisation to high risk groups. It was difficult to know without looking at the wider context whether these findings indicate differences in local health service policy or deficiencies in local authority standards of care.

A different problem was encountered when attempts were made to assess whether girls between the ages of 10 and 15 had received the rubella vaccination. At the initial assessment, 42% were identified as having received the vaccination and 5% as requiring it. However 37% of the respondents left this question blank and in 16% of cases the social worker did not know if the young person needed the vaccination. Further complications arose in that, at the second assessment, 42% of the original group of young people had changed to the over 16 Record where this question was not included and were lost from the analysis, while others aged nine at the first assessment had now graduated to the 10-15 year-old Record, the only one which covered this issue. Thus, care has to be taken to ensure that the Record design and the wording of questions do not distort the results.

These illustrations suggest that caution should be taken in making other interpretations of aggregated data. In the example of the rubella vaccination, it was noted that information was not available for over half the cases. Lack of evidence can make it difficult to understand what the implications are for policy and practice: if missing data are excluded, the results could be interpreted as showing that a high proportion of children have been vaccinated, whereas if the missing data are included and assumed to represent negative answers, the figure obtained may underestimate the number who are protected.

Conclusion

This chapter has demonstrated how issues of concern for individual children can be aggregated and used to change policies and to improve practice. Given the sophistication of the Assessment and Action Records, aggregating and analysing the data obtained from their application are relatively straightforward tasks. The *Looking After Children Management and Implementation Guide* gives further guidance as to how this might be done. However, the interpretation of data has been shown to be a more difficult problem. Too much focus on one area of a child's life obscures other developmental issues and presents in stark black and white a picture which should more accurately be shown in shades of grey. Aggregated data need careful interpretation. The experience of this implementation exercise suggests that it is important for someone in each agency to be designated and appropriately trained to interpret the material and evaluate the results so that services can be improved for the benefit of children. This book opened with Southey's question 'what good came of it at last?' Only a combination of accurate data and sensitive interpretation will give a proper answer.

Summary Points

1. *Looking After Children* enables local authorities to collect information about individuals and groups of children. This information can be used to indicate changes over time.

2. The information obtained from using the Assessment and Action Records can be used for wider monitoring of services and interventions. For example, all the looked after children who were aged 16 and over had received health education but some undesirable behaviours such as smoking, excessive drinking and drug abuse persisted. Information from the Records could be used, therefore, to monitor the effectiveness of health education for looked after children.

3. Although managers need information about deficiencies in child care services in order to plan improvements, the information collected can and should be used to demonstrate strengths as well as weaknesses.

4. Comparisons of aggregated data collected at different points in time need to be made carefully. Like cases need to be compared, individual and group characteristics must not be confused and account must be taken of missing responses, the wording of questions and the content of the Record.

5. Agencies planning to aggregate the data need to ensure that a member of staff is adequately trained to interpret the evidence produced by the application of the materials.

Chapter 10

Conclusions

In the late 1970s, there was a considerable expansion in the amount of research into children 'in care'. The Department of Health commissioned a set of inter-related projects, as did the Economic and Social Research Council. All of these studies highlighted weaknesses in the services local authorities provided. Children became isolated during their stay 'in care' and standards of professional practice and record-keeping were unsatisfactory. This situation led Roy Parker, in his book *Caring for Separated Children*, published in 1980, to pose the question, can the state parent? In the ensuing debate, improvements were suggested in early prevention and permanency planning, but little objective evidence was offered, particularly on the long-term development of separated children and the outcomes of interventions. Many studies provided outcome information but the measures used tended to be very specific, for example, reconviction rates for young offenders, placement stability or length of time 'in care'. There was insufficient information to answer important policy questions, such as how to strike the correct balance between universal and specialist services. Moreover, in some areas of children's lives, such as health and education, hardly anything was known. The need for reliable methods of assessing the outcomes of interventions was clear. Fashioning a replicable methodology would help generate reliable evidence and encourage comparisons between different evaluations.

As a result, the Working Party on Child Care Outcomes explored the concept of outcome and how it might be assessed (Parker *et al*,1991). The approach adopted rested on ideas of good parenting as illuminated by research. The study was an advance in that it linked the abstract concept of outcome to professional practice. Research knowledge was employed to develop instruments that could assess children's needs and chart their progress.

The Assessment and Action Records assume high standards of care which are child-centred and age-specific; changes in progress are monitored in seven areas of children's lives. A link is assumed between input and outcome and children are assessed by asking not only how far they are progressing along each developmental dimension but also how far their potential is realised. Many other benefits follow from using these materials: they set an agenda for social work interactions with children, they help practitioners to identify shortfalls in the service provided and encourage them to plan and monitor improvements, they clarify and allocate professional responsibilities. In addition the materials produce information of different kinds, for example on individual children's development, and aggregated data about the progress and experiences of all those separated from home. Thus an innovative method of disseminating research messages to practitioners can be put in place.

The working party's deliberations coincided with significant changes in child care law and the administration of public services. The implementation of the *Children Act 1989* was imminent, legislation that was markedly to change ideas of parenting and the state's role in the family life of vulnerable children. Concepts of enduring parental responsibility and shared care were intrinsic to the legislation. In addition, there was a wider movement throughout the western world for public agencies to be more accountable. Evaluations of professional performance were increasingly demanded, a development that was already pressing in health and education services by the time the *Looking After Children* project was planned.

The subsequent development of the *Looking After Children* materials has been influenced by these wider changes. In Chapter Six, we saw how the practical applications of the ideas on outcome went well beyond the original aim of providing a comparative research instrument. In the course of the work, we learned much about the problems of converting a theoretical idea into a practical tool which was accessible to fieldworkers and carers and could be used as an integral part of their work. As was shown in Chapters Two and Five, abstract research cannot be applied to practice without the involvement of the professionals concerned. In addition, the support of policy makers in central and local government is essential for widespread implementation. Clearly the tripartite arrangement between researchers, policy makers and practitioners under-pinned the development of this project and facilitated its success. The publication of a regular bulletin was seen as a useful way of strengthening links between all those involved.

But the wider the debate, the greater the need for compromise. The assessment materials had to take into account, for example, the bureaucratic features of social services, such as case review points, and the responsibilities of senior managers to provide practical guidance for their staff. Practitioners also emphasised the need to respect the varied characteristics of children looked after, particularly their ethnic affiliation and special needs. This became manifest in fashioning the materials to meet the needs of children with disabilities. Although the revised materials are still based on the ideas developed by the working party, recent versions are fuller and broader in scope. In addition, a training resources pack for those using the materials and a computer programme to record essential information have been produced.

As the project seeks to meet the expectations of a wide audience, those with specific child care interests, whether professionals, researchers or clients, will perceive some weaknesses in the materials. These criticisms and the ways in which they have been met by the research team have been discussed in the early chapters of this book. Nevertheless, as it is now obligatory for local authorities to monitor decisions about children and achieve optimum standards, attentive monitoring and record-keeping are essential. *Looking After Children* offers an effective and flexible assessment and evaluation system, based on research and theories of child and adolescent development. The materials have now been tested widely in the field. It is intended to implement the *Looking After Children* system in full from April 1995. In the following twelve months some 40 local authorities in England and Wales will begin to use the materials. This next stage of the implementation programme has been informed by the findings from the research and development work described in this book.

The lessons from the initial implementation are twofold. Firstly, the breadth and size of *Looking After Children* means that the materials are more easily introduced if the local authority bureaucracy is sympathetic to the change. In the case study, described in Chapter Seven, the authority devoted a great deal of resources to child care and to creating an ethos of high standards. This helped in getting the project off the ground. The interest and support of managers helped the research survive departmental reorganisations; decisions to implement the materials throughout the authority will facilitate the regular assessment of children who frequently move from one place to another. The local authority also made a special effort to incorporate the new system into its other monitoring procedures such as juvenile justice and child protection; it also instituted special training.

Secondly, although *Looking After Children* seeks to reduce the tendency for child care decisions to reflect moral and pragmatic concerns by introducing research evidence and, *de facto*, a consumer view into the decision process, the implementation raised new moral and practical questions. It became apparent that it was impossible to work in a moral vacuum, a situation reflected in practitioners' questions about the ideological assumptions on which the instruments were based. The Assessment and Action Records clearly take a positive view of partnership and promote a style of interaction between professionals and clients. Implicit is the belief that social workers insufficiently monitor their work and that agencies should produce sophisticated statistics. The materials assume that accurate information, however unwelcome it may be, is the key to effective policy development.

As a major research and development exercise, *Looking After Children* has important messages for child care policy and practice. It provides a broad view of the child's development and employs a longitudinal perspective, integrating both in a single information system. As well as facilitating a comprehensive assessment of children's needs, the use of the materials should make it easier for practitioners to see links between different aspects of children's lives, such as school, family and social relations. The concern with the child's spiritual and moral growth is also important, particularly the sensitivity that the materials show to the cultural context in which children grow up.

Naturally, some weaknesses and omissions will become apparent as the materials are used. The emphasis on the individual, for example, may deflect attention from sibling relationships and the way that these can influence plans for particular children. Similarly, observers may argue that some of the structural factors which can limit the economic and social opportunities of disadvantaged adolescents have been ignored. But whatever criticisms arise, it is important to emphasise that *Looking After Children* is optimal for understanding the needs of looked after children because of its theoretical coherence and relative simplicity.

Central to the discussion in this book has been the relationship between research and development. While the benefits of using *Looking After Children* for child care policy and practice are apparent, other issues are less clear. Some very practical questions have been raised, such as who needs what information and at what time? Or, even more down to earth, what do practitioners do with all the data that are generated? Other issues are more abstract; for instance, if the introduction of *Looking After Children* is an effective way of improving services, how does it differ from other methods, such as a quick audit or swift inspection?

The book has highlighted some of the tensions between ideas and practice. It shows how difficult it is to apply what seem generally excellent ideas to specific situations and how practical problems can intervene. As we saw in Chapter Five, much child care practice is challenged by introducing the ideas of monitoring and outcome but the ability of practitioners to change in a context of limited resources has been questioned by the trial implementations.

The broad scope of *Looking After Children* means that, although it has many uses and functions, it will inevitably fail to satisfy everyone's needs. The way the materials changed from a research instrument to a practice tool indicates this difficulty and we have seen that compromise was necessary. There was always a danger that if the materials had been influenced only by research, they would probably have never been implemented. The way in which questions of viability increasingly jostled with research issues as the project developed has been a particularly interesting feature of this exercise.

The welcome given to *Looking After Children* by practitioners and carers will depend not only on its attractive format and the success of the implementation programme but on changes in child care generally. It is probably a cliché to say that social work will become more professional but it is likely to have to respond to the needs of children and young people more sensitively. This approach would require the disaggregation of global categories of client groups or presenting problems, such as offending or abuse, and more attention to research findings which link input and outcome. Care plans and interventions will become more specific, a process which *Looking After Children* clearly facilitates.

But if child care develops, so must *Looking After Children* and it seems opportune to ask, what comes next? Naturally, there will be continual revision of the materials as they are tested and in the light of the evidence they provide. Questions will need to be reworded and items replaced in the light of new and more accurate indicators emerging from research and changing social attitudes on children's problems and needs.

At the moment, child care interventions tend to deal with almost everything. This is reflected in the structure of *Looking After Children* and in its attempt to set general conditions that are thought likely to help looked after children lead a fulfilling adult life. Practitioners and carers are encouraged to reduce the barriers that limit children's opportunities as well as to extend the positive aspects of young people's situations. As the focus of child care increasingly incorporates specific remedies within a general welfare context, the *Looking After Children* materials may need to be complemented by other instruments which, although applied and interpreted in the context of the child's whole experience, relate to one issue. Practice aids such as checklists and predictive scales are likely to be a feature of research and development in the future.

While *Looking After Children* represents a change in child care practice, it is important to keep the momentum going. It would be unfortunate if *Looking After Children* became a belief system in its own right and fossilised. It needs continually to take account of changes in child care knowledge, such as better predictions, greater awareness of the factors associated with different outcomes and findings from studies that use controls and experiments. Such developments will be generally good for child care. Rather than undermining *Looking After Children* they should act as a source of stimulation.

Finally, we need to revise our ideas if services for children and young people are to improve. The move required is from development work that devises the materials from research, tests their viability and implements them, to a further stage in which the effects of the changes on outcomes for children are scientifically assessed. This book has described how the original concern with outcome tended to be overlooked as other issues arose. It is one thing to show that *Looking After Children* is a useful approach to the problem of outcome assessment, to demonstrate that it can be successfully implemented is more difficult. However, the ultimate test of *Looking After Children* is not whether it will be adopted by social services departments but whether it can improve outcomes for looked after children.

Appendix One

MEMBERSHIP OF RESEARCH TEAMS, ADVISORY GROUPS AND WORKING PARTIES

RESEARCH AND DEVELOPMENT TEAM

Harriet Ward, Dartington Social Research Unit

Hilary Corrick, seconded to DSRU from Hampshire Social Services Department

Sonia Jackson, University of Swansea

Debbie Jones, seconded to DSRU from Oxfordshire Social Services Department

Anne Mason, Dartington Social Research Unit

Sue Moyers, Dartington Social Research Unit

TRAINING RESOURCES TEAM

Sonia Jackson, University of Swansea

Sue Kilroe, University of Bristol

COMPUTER DEVELOPMENT TEAM, SOCIAL SERVICES
RESEARCH AND DEVELOPMENT UNIT, UNIVERSITY OF
BATH

Andrew Kerslake

Paul Goldsworthy

Nick Gould

Alan Gregory

Lorraine Simpson

Ellen Simms

Chris Taylor

JOINT STEERING GROUP

Wendy Rose, Department of Health, Social Services
Inspectorate (Chair)

Jim Brown, Department of Health, Social Services Inspectorate
(Secretariat)

Hilary Corrick, Hampshire Social Services Department

David Crosbie, Department of Health, Social Services
Inspectorate

Carolyn Davies, Department of Health, Research and
Development Division

Peter Goldblatt, Department of Health, Statistics Division

Rupert Hughes, Department of Health, Community Services
Division

Elizabeth Hunter Johnston, Department of Health, Community
Services Division

Sonia Jackson, University of Swansea

Debbie Jones, Oxfordshire Social Services Department

Helen Jones, Department of Health, Social Services Inspectorate

Andrew Kerslake, Social Services Research and Development Unit, University of Bath

Mike Laxton, Social Work Services Inspectorate, Scottish Office

Jeremy Lissamore, Department of Health, Medical Division

Michael Little, Dartington Social Research Unit

Anne Mason, Dartington Social Research Unit

David Matthews, Department of Health, Community Services Division

Kevin Mount, Dartington Social Research Unit

Sue Moyers, Dartington Social Research Unit

David Quinton, University of Bristol (formerly at Institute of Child Psychiatry, University of London)

Jane Scott, Department of Health, Research and Development Division (Secretariat)

Sue Shepherd, Department of Health, Medical Division

Ruth Sinclair, National Children's Bureau

Chris Walker, Social Services Inspectorate, Northern Ireland Office

Harriet Ward, Dartington Social Research Unit

Trish White, Social Services Inspectorate, Welsh Office

TRAINING ADVISORY GROUP

Wendy Rose, Department of Health, Social Services Inspectorate (Chair)

Jim Brown, Department of Health, Social Services Inspectorate (Secretariat)

Margaret Boushel, University of Bristol

Hilary Corrick, Hampshire Social Services Department

Carolyn Davies, Department of Health, Research and Development Division

Len Goldstone, Open University

Sonia Jackson, University of Swansea

Debbie Jones, Oxfordshire Social Services Department

Helen Jones, Department of Health, Social Services Inspectorate

Sue Kilroe, University of Bristol

Ivan Limmer, Department of Health, Social Services Inspectorate

David Matthews, Department of Health, Community Services Division

Imelda Murphy, Kensington and Chelsea Social Services Department

Claire Roskill, CCETSW

Jane Scott, Department of Health, Research and Development Division

Harriet Ward, Dartington Social Research Unit

COMPUTER ADVISORY GROUP

Carolyn Davies, Department of Health, Research and Development Division (Chair)

Alison Campbell, Department of Health, Social Services Inspectorate

David Glasgow, Department of Psychology, Highroyd's Hospital, Leeds

Peter Goldblatt, Department of Health, Statistics Division

Helen Jones, Department of Health, Social Services Inspectorate

Andrew Kerslake, Social Services Research and Development Unit, University of Bath

Michael Little, Dartington Social Research Unit

David Matthews, Department of Health, Community Services Division

Jane Scott, Department of Health, Research and Development Division (Secretariat)

Chris Taylor, Social Services Research and Development Unit, University of Bath

Harriet Ward, Dartington Social Research Unit

CONSULTATION GROUP OF HEALTH

Harriet Ward, Dartington Social Research Unit (Chair)

Kate Billingham, Carlton Family Health Centre, Nottingham

Maddy Blackburn, Community Paediatric Research Unit, Chelsea and Westminster Hospital

Margaret Buttigieg, Health Visitors Association

Paul Bywaters, Coventry University

Maura Connolly, Health Visitors Association

Sue Crook, Dartington Social Research Unit (Secretariat)

Alan Emond, Institute of Child Health, University of Bristol

Jenny Gray, Department of Health, Social Services Inspectorate

Helen Jones, Department of Health, Social Services Inspectorate

Sue Kilroe, University of Bristol

Felicity Leenders, Department of Health, Nursing Division

Ivan Limmer, Department of Health, Social Services Inspectorate

Rebecca Mann, Health Needs of Children in Care Research Project, Redditch

Anne Mason, Dartington Social Research Unit

Carol Mattock, Walpole House, Children and Families Mental Health Centre, Ealing

Marion Miles, Parkside Health Trust, Westbourne Green

Jane Naish, Royal College of Nursing

Heather Payne, Lansdowne Hospital, Cardiff

Simon Ramsden, Wytham Hall Sick Bay for the Homeless, Maida Vale

Jane Scott, Department of Health, Research and Development Division (Secretariat)

Sue Shepherd, Department of Health, Medical Division

CONSULTATION GROUP ON EDUCATION

Harriet Ward, Dartington Social Research Unit (Chair)

John Bald, Who Cares? Trust

Sue Crook, Dartington Social Research Unit (Secretariat)

Audrey Curtis, formerly at London Institute of Education

Cedric Davies, OFSTED

Cedric Dowe, Department of Education

Howard Firth, Hampshire Social Services Department

Helen Jones, Department of Health, Social Services Inspectorate

Chris Hall, Dartington Social Research Unit (formerly at National Foundation for Educational Research)

Sonia Jackson, University of Swansea

Debbie Jones, Oxfordshire Social Services Department

Sue Kilroe, University of Bristol

Anne Mason, Dartington Social Research Unit

Frances Megan, Who Cares? Trust

Jane Scott, Department of Health, Research and Development Division (Secretariat)

Barbara Tizard, Thomas Coram Research Unit

CONSULTATION GROUP ON LEGAL AND ETHICAL ISSUES

Harriet Ward, Dartington Social Research Unit (Chair)

Peter Clarke, Oxfordshire County Council, County Solicitor's Office

Hilary Corrick, Hampshire Social Services Department

Sue Crook, Dartington Social Research Unit (Secretariat)

Deborah Cullen, British Agencies for Adoption and Fostering

Andy Hosking, Leeds City Council Legal Services Agency

Debbie Jones, Oxfordshire Social Services Department

Helen Jones, Department of Health, Social Services Inspectorate

Sue Kilroe, University of Bristol

Judith Masson, School of Law, University of Warwick

Kate Morris, Family Rights Group

Sue Moyers, Dartington Social Research Unit

John Page, Kensington and Chelsea Social Services Department

Sue Pickering, Department of Health, Solicitors' Division

Jane Scott, Department of Health, Research and Development Division (Secretariat)

Ruth Sinclair, National Children's Bureau

Philip Thomson, Essex County Council, Chief Executive and Clerk's Department

WORKING PARTY ON PLANS AND REVIEWS

Hilary Corrick, Hampshire Social Services Department (Chair)

Sally Cosstick, Hampshire Social Services Department

Sue Crook, Dartington Social Research Unit (Secretariat)

Celia Dunkley, North Yorkshire Social Services Department

Anne Edwards, Kensington and Chelsea Social Services Department

Diane Ferry, Hampshire Social Services Department

Patricia Grainger, North Yorkshire Social Services Department

Bridget Griffin, Brent Social Services Department

John Griffin, Brent Social Services Department

Helen Jones, Department of Health, Social Services Inspectorate

Andrew Kerslake, Social Services Research and Development Unit, University of Bath

Alistair Kidd, Greenwich Social Services Department

Anne Mason, Dartington Social Research Unit

Malcolm McKenzie, Kensington and Chelsea Social Services Department

Imelda Murphy, Kensington and Chelsea Social Services Department

Angela Phillips, Hampshire Social Services Department

Malcolm Phillips, Kensington and Chelsea Social Services Department

Jenny Polyblank, Hampshire Social Services Department

Gita Sharma, Brent Social Services Department

Sheila Simpson, Kensington and Chelsea Social Services Department

Harriet Ward, Dartington Social Research Unit

Stephen Whitmore, Greenwich Social Services Department

David Worlock, Kensington and Chelsea Social Services Department

Beverley Young, Hampshire Social Services Department

Specific advice from: Jenny Clifton, University of Sussex

Bernie Dornan, Birmingham Social Services Department

Geoff James, Department of Health, Social Services Inspectorate

Roger Grimshaw, National Children's Bureau

Julia Partridge, Birmingham Social Services Department

Ruth Sinclair, National Children's Bureau

Pat Verity, National Foster Care Association

WORKING PARTY ON CHILDREN WITH DISABLILITIES

Debbie Jones, Oxfordshire Social Services Department (Chair)

Jonathon Fisher, Oxfordshire Social Services Department

Jo Herkes, Kensington and Chelsea Social Services Department

Margaret Jack, Kensington and Chelsea Social Services Department

Angela Kerswell, Hampshire Social Services Department

Maureen Levinson, Hampshire Social Services Department

Anne Mason, Dartington Social Research Unit

Philippa Russell, Council for Disabled Children

Maris Stratulis, Brent Social Services Department

Sally Watts, Oxfordshire Social Services Department (Secretariat)

Colin Wilson, Cleveland Social Services Department

Specific advice from Peter Smith, Department of Health, Social Services Inspectorate

WORKING PARTY ON THE *LOOKING AFTER CHILDREN* COMPUTER SYSTEM

Peter Goldblatt, Department of Health, Statistics Division (Chair)

Frank Binks, ICL

Mick Collinson, ICL

Evelyn Fernando, Berkshire Social Services Department

Stan Groves, Wandsworth Social Services Department

Sally Harris, Buckinghamshire Social Services Department

Andrew Kerslake, Social Services Research and Development Unit, University of Bath

John King, ICL

Simon Lowles, Buckingham Social Services Department

Gina Middleton, Sheridan Systems

Mike Monk, East Sussex Social Services Department

Peter O'Hara, OLM Systems

John O'Shea, Department of Health, Statistics Division (Secretariat)

Joyce Phillips, Redbridge Social Services Department

Sandie Slater, Berkshire Social Services Department

Chris Taylor, Social Services Research and Development Unit, University of Bath

Alan Warren, Richmond Social Services Department

Appendix Two

Demonstration Copy of the Original Assessment and Action Record, Education Dimension, 5–9 year-olds

E	**Education**	**5–9 years**

The questions in this section are designed to make sure that the child's educational attainments are average or above and that s/he acquires special skills and interests and takes a full part in school activities

E 1 How well is the child doing at school?

Reading:

☐ Poor   ☐ Below average   ☐ Average
☐ Above average   ☐ Excellent   ☐ Don't know

Writing:

☐ Poor   ☐ Below average   ☐ Average
☐ Above average   ☐ Excellent   ☐ Don't know

Mathematics:

☐ Poor   ☐ Below average   ☐ Average
☐ Above average   ☐ Excellent   ☐ Don't know

If the child is not doing well, i.e. poor performance in all or some of these areas, what further action will be taken?

Who will take it?

☐ Parent   ☐ Social Worker   ☐ Foster Carer
☐ Residential Worker   ☐ Other   ☐ No action needed

Explanation for lack of information or no action

E 2 How often does the child go to a library or bring a book home from school?

☐ Once a week   ☐ Once a month   ☐ Less than once a month

☐ Don't know

If less than once a week, what further action will be taken?

Who will take it?

☐ Parent   ☐ Social Worker   ☐ Foster Carer
☐ Residential Worker   ☐ Other   ☐ No action needed

Explanation for lack of information or no action

E 3 Who provides help with school work?

☐ Parent ☐ Social Worker ☐ Foster Carer

☐ Residential Worker ☐ Other ☐ No-one

☐ Don't know

If no-one or don't know, who will take responsibility for helping in the future?

☐ Parent ☐ Social Worker ☐ Foster Carer

☐ Residential Worker ☐ Other ☐ No action needed

Explanation for lack of information or no action

E 4 Whose responsibility is it to discuss the child's school progress with teachers and record decisions taken?

☐ Parent ☐ Social Worker ☐ Foster Carer

☐ Residential Worker ☐ Other ☐ No-one

☐ Don't know

If no-one or don't know, who will take responsibility in the future?

☐ Parent ☐ Social Worker ☐ Foster Carer

☐ Residential Worker ☐ Other ☐ No action needed

Explanation for lack of information or no action

E 5 Who attends school events and parents' evenings?

☐ Parent ☐ Social Worker ☐ Foster Carer

☐ Residential Worker ☐ Other ☐ No-one

☐ Don't know

If no-one attends, who will go in the future?

☐ Parent ☐ Social Worker ☐ Foster Carer

☐ Residential Worker ☐ Other ☐ No action needed

Explanation for lack of information or no action

E 6 Does the child go to school regularly?

☐ Yes ☐ No ☐ Don't know

If no or don't know, what further action will be taken?

Who will take it?

☐ Parent ☐ Social Worker ☐ Foster Carer

☐ Residential Worker ☐ Other ☐ No action needed

Explanation for lack of information or no action

E 7 What non-classroom activities has the
child participated in?
(e.g. outings/clubs/sports)

If none, what further action will be taken?

Who will take it?

☐ Parent   ☐ Social Worker   ☐ Foster Carer

☐ Residential Worker   ☐ Other   ☐ No action needed

Explanation for lack of information or no action

E 8 Which of the following has the child
learnt to do?

Swim   ☐ Yes   ☐ No   ☐ Don't know

Ride a bicycle   ☐ Yes   ☐ No   ☐ Don't know

Begin to play a musical instrument   ☐ Yes   ☐ No   ☐ Don't know

Does the child have other skills or
hobbies, not detailed above? Specify:

What further action is needed to encourage these?

Who will take it?

☐ Parent   ☐ Social Worker   ☐ Foster Carer

☐ Residential Worker   ☐ Other   ☐ No action needed

Explanation for lack of information or no action

E 9   Have learning disabilities been noted?

☐ Yes   ☐ No   ☐ Don't know

If so, have these been recorded?

☐ Yes   ☐ No   ☐ Don't know

☐ Not applicable

If disabilities have been recognised, what extra help is the child receiving?

What further action is needed?

Who will take it?

☐ Parent   ☐ Social Worker   ☐ Foster Carer

☐ Residential Worker   ☐ Other   ☐ No action needed

Explanation for lack of information or no action

E 10   How many unscheduled changes of school has the child experienced since the involvement of the social services department? (see guidelines)

☐ Number   ☐ Don't know

Have all changes of school been recorded?

☐ Yes   ☐ No   ☐ Don't know

What action has been taken to encourage continuity?

Who will take further action if necessary?

☐ Parent   ☐ Social Worker   ☐ Foster Carer

☐ Residential Worker   ☐ Other   ☐ No action needed

Explanation for lack of information or no action

**HAVE THE FOLLOWING AIMS
BEEN ACHIEVED?**

AE1   The child's educational
attainments are average or above

All well below
average | | All well above
average

AE 2   The child is acquiring special
skills and interests

None | | Many

AE 3   The child is participating fully in
school activities

Not at all | | Fully

AE 4   The child is favourably regarded
by teachers

Very
unfavourably | | Very favourably

NOTE IF ANYBODY DISAGREES
WITH THIS ASSESSMENT

Demonstration Copy of the Revised Assessment and Action Record, Education Dimension, 5–9 year-olds

EDUCATION

The questions in this section are designed to make sure that the child is being encouraged to develop his/her academic potential, acquire special skills and interests and take a full part in school activities; and that efforts are made to see that s/he is happy at school. **You might find it helpful to refer to the child's most recent school report when completing this section.**

Person with Educational Responsibility

Sometimes a teacher with pastoral responsibilities, an education social worker, education liaison officer or an education welfare officer will help to make sure that arrangements for the child's education are properly carried out. If someone like this is helping the child, please write down their name here:

Name:

Position (education):

Name:

Position (social services department):

Later in this section the term 'Person with educational responsibility' will be used to describe them.

E1 Does the child go to:

	Full time	Part time	If part time, how many hours each week?
Mainstream day school	☐	☐	☐ Hours
Special unit or class in a mainstream day school	☐	☐	☐ Hours
Special day school	☐	☐	☐ Hours
Pupil referral unit (PRU)	☐	☐	☐ Hours
Home tuition	☐	☐	☐ Hours
Residential special school	☐	☐	☐ Hours
Other (eg private boarding school) please specify	☐	☐	☐ Hours

Pupil referral units (PRUs) are for children and young people who, for a variety of reasons, including very disruptive behaviour or exclusion from school, cannot receive suitable education within the usual school system.

No school place available ☐

Don't know ☐

Is the child receiving education appropriate to his/her needs?
☐ Yes   ☐ Currently being assessed
☐ No   ☐ Don't know

The child's attendance last term was as follows:

S/he could have attended [ ] sessions

but actually attended [ ] sessions

S/he was absent for [ ] sessions

and of those [ ] sessions

were authorised absence because s/he had a genuine reason for not attending school.

What were the reasons for unauthorised absence?

Has the child been excluded from school in the last term?
☐ Yes, permanently   ☐ Yes, temporarily
☐ No   ☐ Don't know

E1 contd

If temporarily excluded, for how many days? ☐☐ days

If permanently excluded, how long is it since the child went to school? ☐☐ years ☐☐ months ☐☐ days

Who will take further action if needed? ☐ No further action needed because

☐ Further action needed but not possible or appropriate at present because

Further action will be taken by:

☐ Parent(s)   ☐ Foster carer(s)
☐ Social worker   ☐ Person with educational responsibility
☐ Residential worker   ☐ Other *(please specify)*

E2 Does the child need help, equipment or adaptations to make sure s/he can get to school, hospital or health centre (eg wheelchair access on bus, allowance for fares)? ☐ Yes   ☐ No   ☐ Don't know   If no, go to E3 →

If yes, please specify:

Who will take further action if needed? ☐ No further action needed because

☐ Further action needed but not possible or appropriate at present because

Further action will be taken by:

☐ Parent(s)   ☐ Foster carer(s)
☐ Social worker   ☐ Person with educational responsibility
☐ Residential worker   ☐ Other *(please specify)*

A child has learning difficulties if s/he finds it much harder to learn than most children of the same age, or if s/he has a disability which makes it difficult to use the normal educational facilities in the area. For example someone may have learning difficulties caused by a physical disability; a problem with sight, hearing or speech; a learning *(contd next page)*

E3 Does the child have a learning difficulty?

☐ No   If no, go to E4 →
☐ Yes   ☐ Currently being assessed   ☐ Don't know

If difficulties have been identified, what extra help is the child getting?

disability eg Down's syndrome; emotional or behavioural problems; a medical or health problem or difficulties with reading, writing, speaking or mathematics. Information about individual education plans and statements of special educational need should be noted on the Essential Information Record or file and updated at each review. The social worker should check that details about specialist learning materials such as the use of a word processor or materials in Braille have also been recorded.

E3 contd

Who will take further action if needed?

☐ No further action needed because

☐ Further action needed but not possible or appropriate at present because

Further action will be taken by:

☐ Parent(s)   ☐ Foster carer(s)
☐ Social worker   ☐ Person with educational responsibility
☐ Residential worker ☐ Other *(please specify)*

E4 What does the child enjoy most at school?

What does the child like least about school?

The average level of achievement in National Curriculum subjects at different ages is:
Level 2 by age 7 (Year 2)
Level 4 by age 11 (Year 6)
Level 6 by age 14 (Year 9)

What level has the child achieved in the National Curriculum core subjects of English, mathematics and science?

☐ Not following the National Curriculum

English Level ☐

Mathematics Level ☐

Science Level ☐

If the child is having difficulties with school work, particularly reading or writing, remedial action should be taken immediately.

Do the child, his/her teacher and carer(s) all think that s/he is doing as well as s/he is able?

	Yes	No	Don't know
Child	☐	☐	☐
Teacher	☐	☐	☐
Parent(s)	☐	☐	☐
Carer(s)	☐	☐	☐

Who will take further action if needed?

☐ No further action needed because

☐ Further action needed but not possible or appropriate at present because

Further action will be taken by:

☐ Parent(s)   ☐ Foster carer(s)
☐ Social worker   ☐ Person with educational responsibility
☐ Residential worker ☐ Other *(please specify)*

These are unplanned changes, not those that everyone has (eg from infants to juniors). All school changes should be noted on the child's Essential Information Record or file. Efforts should be made to organise transport so that children do not have to change school if they change placement.

E5 How many times has the child had an unscheduled change of school since s/he was five?

Number ☐☐   ☐ Don't know

Who will take further action if needed?

☐ No further action needed because

[ ]

☐ Further action needed but not possible or appropriate at present because

[ ]

Further action will be taken by:

☐ Parent(s)   ☐ Foster carer(s)
☐ Social worker   ☐ Person with educational responsibility
☐ Residential worker   ☐ Other (please specify)

[ ]

E6 Does the child read for pleasure?

☐ Yes, comics   ☐ Yes, magazines or newspapers
☐ Yes, books   ☐ No, but would like to
☐ No, not interested in reading   ☐ Don't know

How many books does the child own?

☐ Over 10   ☐ 6–10
☐ 1–5   ☐ None
☐ Don't know

How often does the child go to a library?

☐ About once a week   ☐ About once a month
☐ Less than once a month   ☐ Don't know

How often does the child bring a book home from school?

☐ Every day   ☐ Some days
☐ Once a week   ☐ Less than once a week
☐ Don't know

Who will take further action if needed?

☐ No further action needed because

[ ]

☐ Further action needed but not possible or appropriate at present because

[ ]

Further action will be taken by:

☐ Child   ☐ Parent(s)
☐ Foster carer(s)   ☐ Social worker
☐ Residential worker   ☐ Person with educational responsibility
☐ Other (please specify)

[ ]

It is important that someone takes an **E7** interest in the child's school work, provides help when appropriate with work brought home, and makes sure that materials such as pens and paper are available. Foster homes and residential units should have reference books such as dictionaries, atlases and encyclopaedias.

Who regularly hears the child read, provides support with maths, spelling and other school work at home and sees that homework is done?

☐ Parent(s)   ☐ Foster carer(s)

☐ Social worker   ☐ Person with educational responsibility

☐ Residential worker ☐ Other *(please specify)*

☐ No-one   ☐ Don't know

Who will take further action if needed?   ☐ No further action needed because

☐ Further action needed but not possible or appropriate at present because

Further action will be taken by:

☐ Parent(s)   ☐ Foster carer(s)

☐ Social worker   ☐ Person with educational responsibility

☐ Residential worker ☐ Other *(please specify)*

This includes school events and **E8** parents' evenings. An adult who is responsible for the child's care should also be present at any health or education reviews.

Whose responsibility is it to discuss the child's progress with teachers and record decisions taken?

☐ Parent(s)   ☐ Foster carer(s)

☐ Social worker   ☐ Person with educational responsibility

☐ Residential worker ☐ Other *(please specify)*

☐ No-one   ☐ Don't know

Who will take further action if needed?   ☐ No further action needed because

☐ Further action needed but not possible or appropriate at present because

Further action will be taken by:

☐ Parent(s)   ☐ Foster carer(s)

☐ Social worker   ☐ Person with educational responsibility

☐ Residential worker ☐ Other *(please specify)*

Local authorities may have funds **E9** available to help children go on school trips. The social worker should be able to find out whether financial help can be provided for a specific outing.

What non-classroom activities (eg school outings/clubs/sports) has the child participated in?

E9 contd

Which of these activities were integrated (ie arranged for children who have a disability or health condition as well as for those who do not)?

Who will take further action if needed?

☐ No further action needed because

☐ Further action needed but not possible or appropriate at present because

Further action will be taken by:

☐ Child   ☐ Parent(s)

☐ Foster carer(s)   ☐ Social worker

☐ Residential worker   ☐ Person with educational responsibility

☐ Other *(please specify)*

E10 Has the child learnt to:

swim?

☐ Yes   ☐ Learning

☐ No   ☐ Don't know

ride a bicycle?

☐ Yes   ☐ Learning

☐ No   ☐ Don't know

Does the child have other skills or hobbies (eg learning to play a musical instrument, sport, chess)? If so, please give details:

Who will take further action if needed?

☐ No further action needed because

☐ Further action needed but not possible or appropriate at present because

Further action will be taken by:

☐ Child   ☐ Parent(s)

☐ Foster carer(s)   ☐ Social worker

☐ Residential worker   ☐ Person with educational responsibility

☐ Other *(please specify)*

Please record details about plans for further action and target dates in the summary at the back of this Record.

ASSESSMENT OF OBJECTIVES: EDUCATION

The following section should be completed by the social worker in consultation with all those people who are responsible for the child's care. There is a space at the end to record disagreements. After this has been done, look at the previous Assessment and Action Record to see how the child has changed.
How far have the following objectives been met?

Objective 1: The child's educational attainments match his/her ability

☐ Performance matches ability   ☐ Performance somewhat below ability

☐ Performance seriously below ability ☐ Don't know

Objective 2: The child is acquiring special skills and interests

☐ Many   ☐ Some

☐ Few   ☐ None

☐ Don't know

Objective 3: The child is participating fully in a wide range of activities both in and out of school

☐ Wide range   ☐ Some activities

☐ Limited range   ☐ No participation

☐ Don't know

Objective 4: The child is happy at school

☐ Always   ☐ Usually

☐ Sometimes   ☐ Never

☐ Does not attend   ☐ Don't know

Views on the assessment of education objectives 1–4

	Agree(s) fully	Agree(s) partially	Disagree(s)	Not consulted
Child	☐	☐	☐	☐
Parent(s)	☐	☐	☐	☐
Foster carer(s)	☐	☐	☐	☐
Residential worker	☐	☐	☐	☐
Social worker	☐	☐	☐	☐
Person with educational responsibility	☐	☐	☐	☐
Other	☐	☐	☐	☐
please specify				

If you do not agree, please give further details. Say who disagrees and why:

Section completed   Day ☐☐   Month ☐☐   Year ☐☐☐☐

Bibliography

Bald B. and Bean J. (forthcoming), *Reading Opportunities for Looked After Children*, London, Who Cares? Trust.

Baldwin N. (1990), *The Power To Care In Children's Homes*, Aldershot, Avebury.

Bamford F. and Wolkind S. (1988), *The Physical and Mental Health of Children in Care: Research Needs*, ESRC.

Banks M., Bates I., Breakwell G., Bynner J., Emler N., Jamieson L. and Roberts K. (1992), *Careers and Identities*, Milton Keynes, Open University Press.

Bebbington A. and Miles J. (1989), 'The background of children who enter local authority care', *British Journal of Social Work*, **19**, 349–368.

Berridge D. (1985), *Children's Homes*, Oxford, Blackwell.

Berridge D. and Cleaver H. (1987), *Foster Home Breakdown*, Oxford, Blackwell.

Biehal N., Clayden J., Stein M. and Wade J. (1992), *Prepared for Living? A Survey of Young People Leaving the Care of Three Local Authorities*, Leeds University.

Bonnerjea L. (1990), *Leaving Care in London*, London Boroughs Children's Regional Planning Committee.

British Standards Institute and Child Accident Prevention Trust (1994), *Accidents in Childhood*, London, British Standards Institute and Child Accident Prevention Trust.

Bruner J. and Haste H. (eds.) (1987), *Making Sense: The Child's Construction of the World*, London, Methuen.

Bullock R., Little M. and Millham S. (1993), *Going Home: The Return of Children Separated from their Families*, Aldershot, Dartmouth.

Cohen S., Tyrrell D. and Smith A. (1991), 'Psychological stress and susceptibility to the common cold', *New England Journal of Medicine*, **325**, 606–612.

Colton M. (1988), *Dimensions of Substitute Child Care: A Comparative Study of Foster and Residential Care Practice*, Aldershot, Avebury.

Colton M., Jackson S., and Heath A. (eds.) (1994), Special Issue on the Education of Children in Need, *Oxford Review of Education*, **20** (3).

Dennis N. and Erdos G. (1993), *Families Without Fatherhood*, London, I.E.A. Health and Welfare Unit.

Department for Education (1994), *The Education of Children Being Looked After by Local Authorities*, Circular 9, 94.

Department of Health (1989), *An Introduction to the Children Act 1989*, London, HMSO.

Department of Health (1991a), *Looking After Children: Trial Pack (Basic Facts Sheet, Plan, Review Form, Assessment and Action Records and Guidelines for Users)*, London, HMSO.

Department of Health (1991b), *Children in the Public Care: A Review of Residential Child Care*, London, HMSO.

Department of Health (1991c), *The Children Act 1989: Guidance and Regulations*, London, HMSO.

Department of Health (1991d), *Patterns and Outcomes in Child Placement: Messages from Current Research and their Implications*, London, HMSO.

Department of Health (1992), *The Health of the Nation: A Strategy for Health in England*, London, HMSO.

Department of Health (1994a), *Services to Disabled Children and Their Families*, London, HMSO.

Department of Health (1994b) *Guidelines on Smoking and Alcohol Consumption in Residential Child Care Establishments* London, HMSO.

Erikson E.H. (1950), *Childhood and Society*, Harmondsworth, Pelican.

Etzioni A. (1975), *The Semi-Profession and Their Organisation*, New York, Free Press.

Falhberg V. (1988), *Fitting the Pieces Together*, London, British Agencies for Adoption and Fostering.

Fitzgerald J. (1987), 'Young people in the care system', *Adoption and Fostering*, **11**, 19–21.

Fletcher-Campbell F. and Hall C. (1990), *Changing Schools? Changing People?: The Education of Children in Care*, London, National Foundation for Educational Research.

Gardner R. (1987), *Who Says? Choice and Control in Care*, London, National Children's Bureau.

Garnett L. (1994), *The Educational Attainments and Destination of Young People Looked After by Humberside*, Report of Directors of Social Services and Education Services, Unpublished paper.

Goodman R. (1994), 'A modified version of the Rutter parent questionnaire including extra items on children's strengths: a research note', *Journal of Child Psychology and Psychiatry*, **35**, 1483–1494.

Grimshaw R. with Berridge D. (1993), *Educating Disruptive Children: Placement and Progress in Residential Special Schools for Pupils with Educational and Behavioural Difficulties*, London, National Children's Bureau.

Hall P., Land H., Parker R. and Webb A. (1975), *Change, Choice and Conflict in Social Policy*, London, Heinemann.

Halsey A.H. (1993), 'Changes in the family', *Children and Society*, **7**, 125–136.

Herbert M. (1993), *Working with Children and the Children Act: A Practical Guide for the Helping Professions*, Leicester, British Psychological Society Books.

Hewitt P. (1993), *About Time: The Revolution in Work and Family Life*, London, Insititute for Public Policy Research in Association with Rivers Oram Press.

Hoghughi M. (1978), *Troubled and Troublesome: Coping with Severely Disturbed Children*, London, Burnett Books.

Home Office, Department of Health, Department of Education and Science and the Welsh Office (1991), *Working Together Under the Children Act 1989: A Guide to Arrangements for Inter-agency Co-operation for the Protection of Children from Abuse*, London, HMSO.

Howe D. (1986), *Social Workers and their Practice in Welfare Bureaucracies*, Aldershot, Gower.

Jackson S. (1989), 'Education of children in care', in Kahan B. (ed), *Child Care Research, Policy and Practice*, London, Hodder and Stoughton, pp. 133–151.

Jackson S. (1994), 'Educating children in residential and foster care', *Oxford Review of Education*, **20**, 267–279.

Janis I. (1972), *Victims of Groupthink*, Boston, Houghton Mifflin.

Johnson G. (1988), 'Process of managing strategic change', *Management Research News*, **11**, 43–46.

Kahan B. (1989), 'The physical and mental health of children in care', in Kahan B. (ed.), *Child Care Research, Policy and Practice*, London, Hodder and Stoughton, pp. 120–132.

Kuhn T. (1970), *The Structure of Scientific Revolutions*, Chicago, University Press.

Lyon C.M. (1991), *The Implications of the Children Act 1989 on Children and Young People with Severe Learning Difficulties*, Keele, Barnardos and University of Keele.

MacVeigh J. (1982), *Gaskin*, London, Cape.

Millham S., Bullock R., Hosie K. and Haak M. (1986), *Lost in Care: The Problem of Maintaining Links Between Children in Care and Their Families*, Aldershot, Gower.

National Children's Home (1991), *NCH Poverty and Nutrition Survey*, London, National Children's Home.

Newson J. and Newson E. (1963), *Patterns of Infant Care in an Urban Community*, London, Allen and Unwin.

Newson J. and Newson E. (1968), *Four Years Old in an Urban Community*, London, Allen and Unwin.

Newson J. and Newson E. (1976), *Seven Years Old in the Home Environment*, London, Allen and Unwin.

O'Neill T. (1981), *A Place Called Hope: Caring for Children in Distress*, Oxford, Blackwell.

Osborn A.F. and Milbank J.E. (1987), *The Effects of Early Education: A Report from the Child Health and Education Study*, Oxford, Oxford University Press.

Owen M. (forthcoming), *Single Parent Adoptions*, University of Bristol.

Packman J., Randall J. and Jacques N. (1986), *Who Needs Care? Social Work Decisions About Children*, Oxford, Blackwell.

Packman J. and Hall C. (1995), *The Implementation of Section 20 of the Children Act 1989*, Dartington Social Research Unit.

Page R. and Clarke C. (eds.) (1977), *Who Cares? Young People in Care Speak Out*, London, National Children's Bureau.

Parker R. (ed) (1980) *Caring for Separated Children: Plans, Procedures and Priorities*, London, Macmillan.

Parker R.A., Ward H., Jackson S., Aldgate J. and Wedge P. (eds.) (1991), *Looking After Children: Assessing Outcomes in Child Care*, London, HMSO.

Payne H. (1992), *Audit of Medical Care of Children Looked After by South Glamorgan*, Unpublished paper.

Peters T. and Waterman R. (1982), *In Search of Excellence: Lessons from America's Best New Companies*, New York, Harper and Row.

Pettigrew A. and Whipp R. (1991), *Managing For Competitive Success*, Oxford, Blackwell.

Quinton D., Pickles A., Maughan B, and Rutter M. (1993), 'Partners, peers and pathways: assortative pairing and continuities in conduct disorder', *Development and Psychopathology*, **5**, 763–783.

Reder P., Duncan S. and Gray M. (1993), *Beyond Blame: Child Abuse Tragedies Revisited*, London, Routledge.

Rowe J., Cain H., Hundleby M. and Keane A. (1989), *Child Care Now*, London, British Agencies for Adoption and Fostering.

Rutter M. (1975), *Helping Troubled Children*, Harmondsworth, Penguin.

Rutter M. and Rutter M. (1994), *Developing Minds: Challenge and Continuity Across the Lifespan*, Harmondsworth, Penguin.

Rutter M., Taylor E. and Hersov L. (1994), *Child and Adolescent Psychiatry* (Third Edition), Oxford, Blackwell Scientific Publications.

Rutter M., Tizard J. and Whitmore K. (eds.) (1970), *Education, Health and Behaviour*, London, Longmans.

Sinclair R. (1984), *Decision Making in Statutory Reviews on Children in Care*, Aldershot, Gower.

Sinclair R and Grimshaw R. (forthcoming), *Plans and Reviews for Looked After Children: Shaping a Framework for Practice. An Interim Research Report*, London, National Children's Bureau.

Stein M. and Carey K. (1986), *Leaving Care*, Oxford, Blackwell.

Stein M. (1990), *Living Out of Care*, Ilford, Barnardos.

Stephenson P. and Behan D. (1993), *The Education of Children in Cleveland's Community Homes*, Unpublished paper.

Tizard B., Blatchford P., Burke J., Farquar C. and Lewis I. (1988), *Young Children at School in the Inner City*, Hove, Lawrence Erlbaum Associates.

Tizard J., Schofield W. and Hewison J. (1982), 'Collaboration between teachers and parents in assisting children's reading', *British Journal of Educational Psychology*, **52**,1–15.

Triseliotis J. (1980), *New Developments in Foster Care and Adoption*, London, Routledge and Kegan Paul.

Triseliotis J. and Russell J. (1984), *Hard to Place: The Outcome of Adoption and Residential Care*, London, Heinemann Educational Books.

Vernon J. and Fruin D. (1986), *In Care: A Study of Social Work Decision-making*, London, National Children's Bureau.

Ward H., Jackson S. and Parker R. (1991), *A Feasibility Study on the Assessment of Outcomes in Child Care*, Interim Report to the Department of Health, University of Bristol.

YMCA (1994), *Gallup Survey*, London, YMCA.

INDEX

Printed in the United Kingdom for HMSO
Dd300655 C40 4/95 9385 2125